Murder in Mississippi

The 1964 Freedom Summer Killings

by Stephen Currie

LUCENT BOOKS
A part of Gale, Cengage Learning

GALE
CENGAGE Learning

Detroit • New York • San Francisco • New Haven, Conn • Waterville, Maine • London

© 2006 Gale, Cengage Learning

For more information, contact
Lucent Books
27500 Drake Rd.
Farmington Hills, MI 48331-3535
Or you can visit our Internet site at gale.cengage.com

LIBRARY OF CONGRESS CATALOGING-IN-PUBLICATION DATA

Currie, Stephen, 1960–
  Murder in Mississippi : the 1964 freedom summer killings / by Stephen Currie.
    p. cm. — (Crime scene investigations series)
  Includes bibliographical references and index.
  ISBN 1-59018-934-5 (alk. paper)
  1. Murder—Mississippi—Neshoba County—History—20th century. 2. Civil rights workers—Crimes against—Mississippi—Neshoba County—History—20th century. 3. Goodman, Andrew, 1943–1964. 4. Chaney, James Earl, 1943–1964. 5. Schwerner, Michael Henry, 1939–1964. 6. Civil rights movements—Mississippi—History—20th century. 7. Mississippi—Race relations—History—20th century—Sources. I. Title. II. Series.
HV6533.M7C87 2006
364.152'309762685—dc22

2005026797

Printed in the United States of America
3 4 5 6 7 12 11 10 09 08

Contents

Foreword

The popularity of crime scene and investigative crime shows on television has come as a surprise to many who work in the field. The main surprise is the concept that crime scene analysts are the true crime solvers, when in truth, it takes dozens of people, doing many different jobs, to solve a crime. Often, the crime scene analyst's contribution is a small one. One Minnesota forensic scientist says that the public "has gotten the wrong idea. Because I work in a lab similar to the ones on *CSI*, people seem to think I'm solving crimes left and right—just me and my microscope. They don't believe me when I tell them that it's the investigators that are solving crimes, not me."

Crime scene analysts do have an important role to play, however. Science has rapidly added a whole new dimension to gathering and assessing evidence. Modern crime labs can match a hair of a murder suspect to one found on a murder victim, for example, or recover a latent fingerprint from a threatening letter, or use a powerful microscope to match tool marks made during the wiring of an explosive device to a tool in a suspect's possession.

Probably the most exciting of the forensic scientist's tools is DNA analysis. DNA can be found in just one drop of blood, a dribble of saliva on a toothbrush, or even the residue from a fingerprint. Some DNA analysis techniques enable scientists to tell with certainty, for example, whether a drop of blood on a suspect's shirt is that of a murder victim.

While these exciting techniques are now an essential part of many investigations, they cannot solve crimes alone. "DNA doesn't come with a name and address on it," says the Minnesota forensic scientist. "It's great if you have someone in custody to match the sample to, but otherwise, it doesn't help. That's the investigator's job. We can have all the great DNA evidence in the world, and without a suspect, it will just sit on the shelf. We've all seen cases with very little forensic evidence get solved by the resourcefulness of a detective."

While forensic specialists get the most media attention today, the work of detectives still forms the core of most criminal investigations. Their job, in many ways, has changed little over the years. Most cases are still solved through the persistence and determination of a criminal detective whose work may be anything but glamorous. Many cases require routine, even mind-numbing tasks. After the July 2005 bombings in London, for example, police officers sat in front of video players watching thousands of hours of closed-circuit television tape from security cameras throughout the city, and as a result were able to get the first images of the bombers.

The Lucent Books Crime Scene Investigations series explores the variety of ways crimes are solved. Titles cover particular crimes such as murder, specific cases such as the killing of three civil rights workers in Mississippi, or the role specialists such as medical examiners play in solving crimes. Each title in the series demonstrates the ways a crime may be solved, from the various applications of forensic science and technology to the reasoning of investigators. Sidebars examine both the limits and possibilities of the new technologies and present crime statistics, career information, and step-by-step explanations of scientific and legal processes.

The Crime Scene Investigations series strives to be both informative and realistic about how members of law enforcement—criminal investigators, forensic scientists, and others—solve crimes, for it is essential that student researchers understand that crime solving is rarely quick or easy. Many factors—from a detective's dogged pursuit of one tenuous lead to a suspect's careless mistakes to sheer luck to complex calculations computed in the lab—are all part of crime solving today.

Freedom Summer 1964

Through the first half of the twentieth century, African Americans were second-class citizens all across the South. By law and by custom, African Americans in these states enjoyed few rights. Blacks were forced to attend inferior schools, usually prevented from voting, and barred from many facilities such as hotels and restaurants. The system of segregation, or separation of the races, was so deeply ingrained into southern life that many whites—and even many blacks—found it unremarkable. "This [was] the way it had always been," recalled a white southerner, speaking of both whites and blacks during his years growing up in South Carolina. "This [was] the way [we] thought it was supposed to be."[1]

But by the 1950s, attitudes among southern blacks were beginning to change. One reason was the experiences of African American troops during World War II. Though segregated from white soldiers throughout the conflict, American black troops had played a vital role in winning the war. When they came home, however, they were dismayed to find that their sacrifices and courage had not changed the realities of segregation and prejudice. White Americans appreciated the hard work of the black soldiers—but not enough to offer African Americans all the rights of citizenship.

Many veterans found this situation intolerable. As one black soldier explained, "I paid my dues over there [that is, fighting in the war], and I'm not going to take this anymore over here."[2] As a consequence, black soldiers returning from the war slowly began to challenge the system of segregation throughout the South. They argued that racial discrimination was wrong, and they demanded that African Americans be allowed to exercise

After serving honorably in World War II, African American soldiers found that they were still treated as second-class citizens when they returned to the United States.

civil rights—the basic rights, such as the right to free speech and the right to vote, that citizens are normally entitled to simply by virtue of being part of a society. Before long, the efforts of these veterans and their supporters had expanded into a new political organization: the civil rights movement.

The Civil Rights Movement

Most historians today see the civil rights movement as among the most influential and important of all American social reforms. Led primarily by southern blacks with significant support from northern whites, the movement dominated newspaper headlines and news broadcasts from the mid-1950s through the early 1970s. Like the World War II veterans who had been among the first to challenge the system, supporters of the civil rights movement pushed for an end to segregation, an increase in the opportunities available to African Americans, and a recognition that civil rights should be extended to members of all races. Civil rights advocates were determined and focused on their goals. As a song popular within the movement put it, "We'll never turn back / Until we've all been freed."[3]

From its beginnings, however, the civil rights movement was a struggle. Throughout most of the South, civil rights activists met with anger and hostility. Many white southerners were staunchly opposed to giving up the system of segregation. That was true of many ordinary citizens; it was even more obviously true of politicians and government officials. Alabama governor George Wallace, for instance, promised cheering supporters in 1963 that his state would never change its ways. "Segregation now," he thundered, "segregation tomorrow . . . segregation forever."[4]

Such hostility was not expressed simply in words. Often, it spilled over into violence. In 1957, for example, when several black students in Little Rock, Arkansas, tried to attend the local "whites-only" high school, they were threatened by angry mobs. Blacks who tried to register to vote ran the risk of being beaten; arsonists destroyed the homes of some African

Americans who were active in the movement. And by 1964, several civil rights advocates had lost their lives at the hands of white racists at various places in the South.

Despite the dangers, the civil rights movement did make significant progress. The beginning of the movement, in fact, is often dated from a great victory: a 1954 Supreme Court ruling that held that segregation of public schools was unlawful. In 1957, Congress approved a limited civil rights act that established some voting rights for African Americans; seven years later, a similar but much more powerful and sweeping law was passed. Throughout the 1950s and 1960s, civil rights activists

African American students who tried to integrate schools in the South were often met by angry crowds. Here, National Guardsmen keep such a crowd in check outside Central High School in Little Rock, Arkansas, in 1957.

used boycotts and other protests to successfully desegregate bus terminals, restaurants, and other facilities open to the public in many southern cities. And the 1963 March on Washington brought hundreds of thousands of movement supporters together in one of the largest protests held in American history.

"Segregation Was King"

Despite the achievements of the movement as a whole, though, there was one part of the South where the civil rights movement, at least at first, experienced virtually no success. That was the state of Mississippi. Well into the 1960s, Mississippi remained as segregationist as ever. Its leaders routinely denied black citizens even the few rights offered to African Americans in other states. Even by the standards of the South, for example, hardly any Mississippi blacks were registered to vote, and only a small percentage of these actually cast ballots. "In Mississippi, in the 1960s," summed up an African American born and raised in the state, "segregation was king, racism the status quo, and bigotry the law."[5]

Certainly, Mississippi was not fertile territory for civil rights activists. More than that, it was dangerous. Among blacks killed in the South for their civil rights advocacy, a disproportionate number had come from Mississippi. Civil rights leader Medgar Evers was shot and killed in 1963 as he stood outside his house in Jackson, the state capital. In 1961, voting rights activist Herbert Lee was murdered in the town of Liberty; Brookhaven resident Lamar Smith suffered the same fate when he tried to register to vote two years later. The effect on civil rights activity was chilling. In the three years after Herbert Lee's death, not one African American in Liberty attempted to register to vote.

In 1964, however, civil rights leaders decided that the time had come for more

By the Numbers

86 PERCENT

Number of African Americans in Mississippi living below the national poverty line in the early 1960s

action. Several influential activists drew up plans for what became known as the Mississippi Freedom Summer. They planned to have several hundred southern blacks and northern whites—many of these college students—pour into the state and take part in activities to help local African Americans. These volunteers would hold voter registration drives, establish community centers, provide job training and tutoring services, and let Mississippi blacks know that there was hope. In the winter of 1964, the first few activists began fanning out across the state, readying the way for what was to follow.

Protesters who advocated increased civil rights for blacks were frequently arrested. A few, like Medgar Evers (pictured), were murdered.

Preparing for Mississippi

That June, the bulk of the Freedom Summer volunteers gathered in Ohio for orientation and training sessions. Movement leaders stressed to the volunteers that the work would be difficult. For many who had never been to the South, indeed, visiting Mississippi would be a kind of culture shock. The state was still overwhelmingly rural, agricultural, and poor. Mississippi trailed the nation in most measures of wealth and comfort. In particular, much of Mississippi's large black population lived in squalor, at least by the standards of the North. "You better get ready for outhouses,"[6] cautioned veteran activist James Forman.

More important, however, the leaders emphasized the dangers of working in Mississippi. "I may be killed, and you may be killed,"[7] Forman said at the orientation. He pointed out that news of the upcoming Freedom Summer project angered many white Mississippians, who thought that the volunteers were simply trying to stir up trouble. As one white resident of the state complained, the activists were bent on "breaking up our

11

Activist leader James Forman warned civil rights workers in Mississippi that they might be attacked or even murdered by whites who saw them as meddling outsiders.

customs . . . that had been respected by people here over the years."[8] Indeed, white Mississippians commonly used war terminology to describe the Freedom Summer plans. The volunteers, they said, were an "army"; their arrival, an "invasion."

If war was intended, then Mississippi was prepared. The size of the state police force was sharply increased in expectation of the influx of volunteers. Authorities in Jackson purchased shotguns, tear gas, and attack dogs. "We're going to be ready for them," promised Jackson's mayor, referring to the volunteers. "They won't have a chance."[9] Elsewhere in the state, sheriff's deputies, ordinary citizens, and white supremacist groups made similar plans.

The two sides were on a collision course. The civil rights activists were determined to bring about social change and establish justice in one of the least progressive states of the Union. Segregationist Mississippians were equally determined to preserve their way of life regardless of the consequences. James Forman had predicted that the Freedom Summer volunteers could expect to encounter violence—perhaps even death—in Mississippi. But not even Forman could have imagined the crime that actually did take place that summer along a lonely road in rural Mississippi—a crime so brutal, so secretive, and so complex that its investigation took more than forty years.

CHAPTER 1

The Disappearance

In early 1964, several months before Freedom Summer was to begin in earnest, a number of civil rights workers began setting up a community center in the town of Meridian, in the east central part of Mississippi. The five-room center, built for the town's sixteen thousand African Americans, formally opened in February. The center boasted a library of ten thousand books, most of them donated by publishing companies in the North. Staffers also offered story hours for children, a Ping-Pong table, sewing classes, information about voter registration, and more. The workers at the center hoped to use the building as a base for Freedom Summer operations. In the meantime, they expected that Meridian's blacks would benefit from the services they were able to offer.

Schwerner and Chaney

One of the people instrumental in setting up the community center was a twenty-four-year-old social worker, Michael (Mickey) Schwerner. Schwerner, a white man who had grown up in suburban New York City, was a warm and vigorous activist who cared deeply about justice and racial harmony. In late 1963, he decided to leave his social work position in New York City and devote his time instead to battling segregation in the southern states. "I have an emotional need," he wrote, "to offer my services in the South. . . . The vocation for the rest of my life is and will be to work for an integrated society."[10] Along with his activist wife, Rita, Mickey Schwerner arrived in Meridian in January 1964.

One of the first people the Schwerners met in Mississippi was James Chaney. Chaney was twenty in early 1964, just a

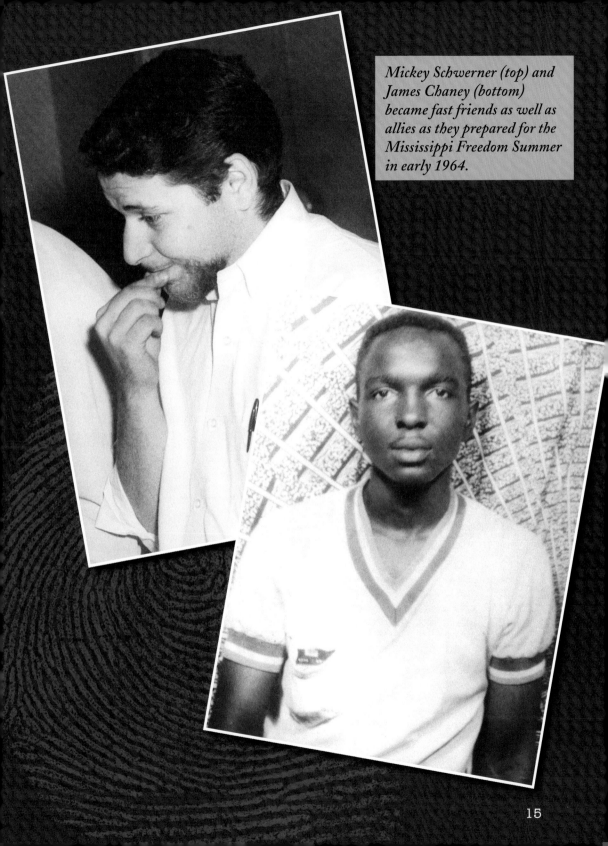

Mickey Schwerner (top) and James Chaney (bottom) became fast friends as well as allies as they prepared for the Mississippi Freedom Summer in early 1964.

few years younger than Mickey and Rita. Other than the rough similarity of ages, however, Chaney's life was different from the Schwerners' in almost every imaginable way. An African American who had been born and raised in Meridian, Chaney had experienced the realities of discrimination firsthand throughout his life. Far from being a college graduate like the Schwerners, Chaney had dropped out of high school in his late teens to work at a succession of odd jobs. Those who spent time with Chaney during this period agreed that he seemed without purpose. As one friend put it, "He knew he wasn't going anywhere."[11]

The civil rights movement, however, changed James Chaney's life. He was brought into the movement in late 1963 when a friend introduced him to an organizer named Matt Suarez. Under Suarez's influence, Chaney became caught up in the movement. He began to devote his energy to canvassing black neighborhoods and giving talks about voter registration. By the time the Schwerners arrived in Meridian, Chaney had become one of the leaders of the city's newly formed civil rights organization.

Despite the differences in their backgrounds, Chaney and Mickey Schwerner soon became close friends and constant companions. "They were like Siamese twins,"[12] Suarez remembered. The two men made an excellent team. Schwerner had a particular gift for organizing people and encouraging them to help the cause; Chaney paved the way for him by introducing him to dozens of blacks who lived in the area. Schwerner's social work training neatly complemented Chaney's firsthand experience of what it meant to be an African American in Mississippi.

Threats and Harassment

At first, the white citizens of Meridian paid little attention to the growing community center and to the projects taken on by Schwerner, Chaney, and their fellow activists. However, the founding of the community center represented a threat to the established way of life in Meridian. The center's focus on providing information on voter registration was sure to upset many local whites. So was the staff's interest in working toward desegregation. Perhaps even more offensive to Meridian's segregationists, however, was the mere existence of a community center staffed by workers such as Schwerner—an outsider from the North—and Chaney, a local African American who did not seem to accept his "place" in society.

Before long, ardent segregationists in and around Meridian realized what was going on at the community center. As Rita Schwerner wryly put it, "As people came to know us better . . . and to know what we were attempting to do, the tension increased."[13] Local blacks who offered to house the Schwerners received threatening phone calls; in at least one case, a white landlord sharply increased the rent for an African American family who took the Schwerners in. Police officers harassed the activists, once jailing Schwerner for three days on charges of blocking a crosswalk. Both Chaney and Schwerner were followed while driving, often by groups of men in cars with license plates either obscured by mud or missing altogether. Eventually, fearing for their safety, the workers stopped driving after dark unless it was absolutely necessary.

The Right to Vote

The Fifteenth Amendment to the U.S. Constitution, adopted in 1870, gave black males the legal right to vote. But despite the law, whites in most parts of the South found ways to prevent blacks from actually casting ballots. Some African Americans were charged poll taxes, money that needed to be paid to local officials before they were permitted to vote; many poor blacks could not afford to make these payments. Others were given literacy tests or quizzed on arcane details of the Constitution. (Whites, as a rule, were subject to neither poll taxes nor tests.) Intimidation was also used to keep blacks from voting. In many communities, blacks who expressed an interest in voting were threatened, and those who tried to vote were beaten or lost their jobs. Despite their legal right to do so, comparatively few southern blacks were voting by the 1960s. It was not until the 1965 Voting Rights Act secured the right of all Americans to vote that African Americans were able to freely practice a right that had been technically granted to them ninety-five years earlier.

Neshoba County sheriff Lawrence Rainey (left), shown here with deputy Cecil Price, had a history of violence against blacks and was bitterly opposed to the civil rights movement.

Despite the threats and the harassment that the civil rights workers faced near the community center, however, the activists stationed there did not consider Meridian the most dangerous part of the region. That dubious honor went to Neshoba County, just to Meridian's northwest. Rural and lightly settled, Neshoba had a white majority along with significant numbers of blacks and Choctaw Indians. To most of the staff members at Meridian's community center, Neshoba—and its county seat, Philadelphia—was to be avoided at all costs. "Many experienced civil rights workers," remarked Rita Schwerner, "refused to enter the territory."[14]

Neshoba County

There were good reasons for civil rights workers to fear Neshoba County. Several white officials there, among them Sheriff Lawrence Rainey and his deputy Cecil Price, were rumored to have ties to a white supremacist organization called the Ku

Klux Klan. The Klan was a secret society that had flourished during the 1920s, before declining in influence and membership. Now, with the increasing call for civil rights, the organization was making a comeback. Bitterly opposed to integration and civil rights, Klan members used terror and violence to intimidate, injure, and even kill those who worked on behalf of African Americans.

Even if the rumors of Klan connections were false, it was certain that Rainey and other county officials were vehemently opposed to civil rights. While campaigning for sheriff in the previous election, for instance, Rainey had argued that he alone of the candidates would be able to "handle the niggers and the outsiders."[15] Rainey also had a history of brutality against African Americans. During the previous few years, he had killed two black men. In both incidents, Rainey claimed self-defense as a justification and was not charged with a crime, but civil rights workers distrusted and feared him nonetheless.

Nor did Neshoba County have a counterweight to the white supremacists. In Meridian, a relatively large and cosmopolitan town by Mississippi standards, some segregationist whites counseled against violent opposition to the civil rights workers. They knew that the eyes of the country would be on Mississippi during the Freedom Summer, and they hoped to present their community and state in the best possible light. But in Neshoba County, few whites spoke up against the views of Rainey, Price, and other powerful officials. Indeed, many citizens proudly echoed the opinions of these men. "Outsiders who come in here and try to stir up trouble," wrote newspaper editor Jack Long Tannehill, "should be dealt with in a manner they won't forget."[16]

Under the circumstances, many civil rights workers feared that they

By the Numbers

26

Number of single-spaced pages listing attacks on and arrests of civil rights workers in Mississippi in 1964

would be arrested, beaten, or killed if they so much as entered Neshoba County. Until Mississippi's larger cities and towns made moves toward greater racial equality, it seemed that there was no hope of overcoming the stubborn racism in rural places like Neshoba. But though some civil rights workers took pains not to cross the county's boundaries for any reason, Chaney and Schwerner felt a strong pull to work with the black population there.

Much of their desire to enter Neshoba County involved the harshness of life for rural Mississippi blacks. In Meridian, African Americans were certainly the victims of prejudice and discrimination, but in several important ways, they were considerably better off than their counterparts in Neshoba County. While voting rights for Meridian blacks were restricted, for instance, some African Americans in that community were able to cast ballots in elections, while not a single African

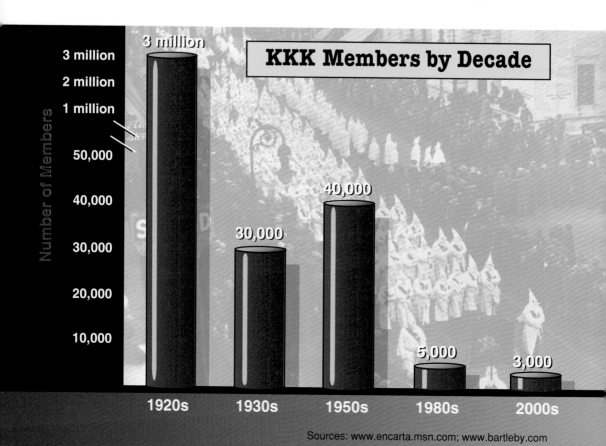

KKK Members by Decade

Number of Members

3 million	
2 million	
1 million	
50,000	

1920s: 3 million
1930s: 30,000
1950s: 40,000
1980s: 5,000
2000s: 3,000

Sources: www.encarta.msn.com; www.bartleby.com

American was even registered in Neshoba County. Schools were better in Meridian; the threat of police brutality was lower; incomes were higher. The assistance of activists such as Chaney and Schwerner was valuable to the African Americans of Meridian, but help was absolutely a necessity to the blacks of Neshoba County.

Schwerner and Chaney also believed that the circumstances of life in Neshoba County would radicalize blacks and encourage them to join the civil rights movement. Most adults in Meridian's African American community, noted Rita Schwerner, "were unwilling to take risks. They pointed to what they [already] had, and they wanted to wait or go slow." But in Neshoba County, she added, African Americans "had less to lose, so the adults were ready to take more risks."[17] For both Chaney and Mickey Schwerner, the prospect of winning enthusiastic converts to their cause seemed worth the potential danger of venturing across Neshoba's borders.

Freedom School

Beginning in February and continuing through the spring of 1964, Chaney and Schwerner made thirty or more trips into Neshoba County. Recognizing the risks involved in these trips, the activists set up procedures and strategies to ensure their safety. When they visited blacks who had telephones, for example, they routinely called headquarters to report on their whereabouts and estimate the time of their return. They kept to the back roads, too, in hopes that county law enforcement officials would not see the community center's distinctive blue station wagon. Finally, much of the organizing work was carried out primarily by Chaney—a black Mississippi native who blended into African American sections of the county far better than Schwerner could hope to do.

The activists began by visiting individual blacks in Neshoba County. They handed out voter registration materials and told local African Americans of the potential benefits of the civil rights movement. But the slow pace of change frustrated

Schwerner and Chaney, and they soon proposed establishing a so-called freedom school in the county. Freedom schools, a common feature of the civil rights movement, were intended to train blacks to stand up for their rights. The proposed Neshoba County school would make it possible for Chaney and Schwerner to reach dozens of African Americans at a time rather than only one or two.

The two men soon decided on a location for the school: Mount Zion Church in Longdale, a Neshoba County community populated entirely by blacks. At a meeting on May 31, Schwerner and Chaney presented their ideas to Mount Zion's congregation. "You have been slaves too long," Schwerner said to the blacks in attendance. "We can help you help yourselves. . . . Meet us here, and we'll train you so you can qualify to vote."[18]

Schwerner's words had the effect he desired. The people of Mount Zion agreed to host the new freedom school. Given the hostility of white county residents to civil rights, not everyone in the congregation was convinced that this was the wisest possible decision. Still, most church members believed that they could not conscientiously do anything else. "God help us, it may be our last act on this earth," one man present at the assembly said later. "But I guess if a man don't try to vote today he ain't *nothing!*"[19]

Terror at Mount Zion

On June 16, just over two weeks after Schwerner spoke at Mount Zion, about ten members of the congregation at-

tended a regular business meeting at the church. Upon leaving the building, they were shocked and dismayed to find about thirty armed white men standing outside. Evidently, white segregationists of Neshoba County had learned of the congregation's willingness to sponsor civil rights activities. It soon became apparent that the armed men believed a pro–civil rights gathering was taking place at the church.

The armed whites allowed the church members to get in their cars and leave the premises. Before the church members had gone far, however, they were overtaken by vehicles driven

Mount Zion Church in Neshoba County was the site of a freedom school intended to educate blacks about their rights.

The Birmingham Church Bombing

Mount Zion was far from the only African American church in the South to be burned or bombed during the civil rights era. On the contrary, destroying black churches was a common tactic used by white supremacists to intimidate African Americans who spoke up for their rights. Churches were a tempting target because they were central to black communities and because they played a pivotal role in supporting and encouraging the battle for civil rights. To destroy a black church, then, not only deprived African Americans of a worship space and a community center but also removed one of the underpinnings of the civil rights movement itself.

The most notorious of these incidents took place on September 15, 1963, when several sticks of dynamite exploded at the Sixteenth Street Baptist Church in Birmingham, Alabama. Though most church bombings occurred at night, the dynamite in the Sixteenth Street church exploded on a Sunday morning when the building was full of worshippers. Four girls were killed in the blast, and more than twenty other people were injured. The bombing shocked many northern whites and galvanized the civil rights movement.

The 1963 bombing of the Sixteenth Street Baptist Church in Birmingham, Alabama, claimed the lives of (left to right) Denise McNair, Addie Mae Collins, Carole Robertson, and Cynthia Wesley. The girls ranged in age from 11 to 14.

College student Andrew Goodman arrived in Mississippi to help with voter registration in June 1964.

by the whites, who forced the church members off the road, yanked them from their cars, and interrogated them about what had been going on in the building. In particular, the white men seemed to want to know where Schwerner was and whether the meeting had touched on the question of voter registration. Even though the whites were satisfied eventually that the gathering had had nothing to do with civil rights, they beat several of the church members—one nearly to the point of unconsciousness—before allowing them to continue on their way home.

The evening, however, was not yet over. An hour or so later, an African American who lived in the area saw five cars speeding down the usually empty road to the church. Two or three hours after that, another local black noticed a strange glow in the sky, but when he tried to investigate, he found a car blocking the road to the church. In the morning, the fears of Neshoba's African American community were realized: Mount Zion had burned to the ground. "All that is now to be seen," wrote one observer soon after the destruction, "are a few bricks and some twisted metal roofing lying where it fell. There is not one piece of timber left, charred or otherwise."[20]

Investigation

No blacks in the area doubted that the fire had been deliberately set. Nor did anyone fail to see that the fire served as a warning to the blacks of Neshoba County and the civil rights workers of Meridian. But whatever the dangers, Mickey Schwerner and James Chaney were not willing to be run out of Neshoba County. On June 21, five days after the church was destroyed, the two made one more trip to Longdale. Their goal was to talk to the people who had been beaten, to gather evidence that

Bud Cole (right), pictured here in 1989 with his wife Beatrice, was one of the Mount Zion Church members who was beaten the night the church was burned.

THIS MEMORIAL IS PRAYERFULLY
AND PROUDLY DEDICATED
TO THE MEMORY OF
JAMES CHANEY
ANDREW GOODMAN
MICHAEL SCHWERNER
WHO GAVE THEIR LIVES IN THE
STRUGGLE TO OBTAIN HUMAN
RIGHTS FOR ALL PEOPLE.

might be useful in finding who was to blame for the church fire, and to determine the future of the movement in Neshoba County.

On this trip, Chaney and Schwerner were joined by a third man. Andrew Goodman, a twenty-year-old white college student from New York City, had finished Freedom Summer training in Ohio only a few days earlier. Like Schwerner, Goodman had a long-standing commitment to social justice; Rita Schwerner described him as a "fine, intelligent, unassuming young man."[21] Arriving in Neshoba County, Schwerner, Chaney, and Goodman picked up Ernest Kirkland, a local man who had been among the first county residents to offer support to the civil rights activists. After visiting the remains of the church, the four men drove to the home of Beatrice and Bud Cole, who had been beaten at the church the night the building burned. Next, they dropped Kirkland off at his own house and started back to Meridian.

No Return

Schwerner had told the staff members at the community center to expect him and his companions around four o'clock that afternoon. But by four thirty, the three men had not yet arrived. Neither had they phoned in to report a change of plans. And as the hours dragged on, they still did not appear. Other activities at the community center were suspended as staffers called their friends and allies throughout the region, looking for some indication that Schwerner, Chaney, and Goodman were safe.

The center workers eventually reached Ernest Kirkland, who said that the three men had left his house several hours before, planning to go straight back to Meridian. Kirkland's information came as a bitter blow to the workers in Meridian. If Kirkland was correct, then there was no reason why the three men should not have been back at the scheduled time. By early evening on June 21, the conclusion was inescapable: Chaney, Schwerner, and Goodman had disappeared.

CHAPTER 2

The Search

Throughout the night of June 21 and the early morning hours of the 22nd, staffers at the community center in Meridian continued to try to locate the three missing men. Just before seven in the morning on the 22nd, staffer Bill Light succeeded in reaching Minnie Herring, the wife of the man who ran the jail in Neshoba County's largest town, Philadelphia. She told Light that the three activists had spent several hours at the Philadelphia jail on the previous day. On their way back to Meridian on the afternoon of the 21st, Herring explained, the three men had been arrested for speeding. However, she added, they had paid a fine of $20 and had been released at about six in the evening.

The news was not reassuring. Uncomfortable as it was for an activist to be in jail, remaining imprisoned was sometimes safer than being set free in an unfamiliar town. In the South, there were often close ties between white supremacist organizations and the law enforcement community. Over the years, several civil rights workers had been released from small-town jails only to be met on the street outside by members of the local Ku Klux Klan. Some of these activists had been severely beaten; others had been killed. Light feared that Herring's husband, working in collusion with Sheriff Rainey and the white supremacists of Neshoba County, had sent Goodman, Schwerner, and Chaney into the clutches of the Ku Klux Klan.

There were, to be sure, three reasons for hope. The first was the timing of the release. Jailers who discharged civil rights workers into the custody of the Klan typically did so after dark, and on June 21, the longest day of the year, six o'clock was long before nightfall. To let the men out so early did not fit the usual pattern. If the men had really been released at the time Minnie Herring claimed, then it was possible that they were not with the Klan. Instead, they might have simply taken refuge with a nearby black family who owned no telephone. If that was the case, the three missing men would probably reappear later on the 22nd.

The second hope involved race. Although violence had long surrounded the civil rights movement, no white civil rights worker had yet been killed. Perhaps the white supremacists were unwilling to kill those of their race; perhaps they feared the possible backlash of white northerners. Whatever the reason, the staffers in Meridian hoped that Neshoba County's white supremacists—if indeed they had taken custody of the three activists—would be unwilling to murder either the two white men or their black companion. Certainly, they reasoned, Klan members would know that the murder of a white worker, or of a black worker accompanied by two whites, would raise a much greater stir than the killing of a black man alone.

And the third hope, finally, involved the way other Americans thought about Mississippi. While the top officials of the state staunchly opposed the civil rights movement and Freedom Summer itself, civil rights veterans knew that these officials were also eager to show their state in a positive light. "Governor [Paul] Johnson doesn't want to see any of us

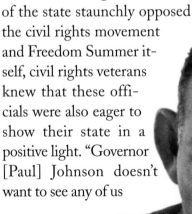

Like many other officials in Mississippi, Governor Paul Johnson viewed the Freedom Summer workers as troublemakers and disapproved of their activities.

getting shot or lynched, because he doesn't want the image of Mississippi damaged," pointed out one activist. "That's the best thing we have going for us."[22] The civil rights workers could only hope that Johnson had communicated his apparent distaste for violence to the white supremacists of Neshoba County.

Spreading the Word

Along with trying to locate Goodman, Schwerner, and Chaney, the Meridian activists also spread the word about the three men's disappearance. If the men were not yet dead, they were probably in serious danger. In that case, the more people who knew about their disappearance, the better the odds that they could be rescued. Consequently, the staffers in Meridian alerted news reporters in northern cities. They spoke to fellow civil rights advocates in other southern towns. They contacted the families of the three missing men and alerted law enforcement officials as well.

When a person disappears, friends and relatives usually begin the search by contacting state and local police forces. However, the men and women who were trying to find Chaney, Schwerner, and Goodman believed that they would get little help from Mississippi officials. The prevailing sentiment among whites in the state, after all, was fervently pro-segregation and anti–civil rights. The mayor of Jackson, the governor of Mississippi, the sheriff of Neshoba County—all had spoken

Civil Rights Deaths by Year

The Civil Rights Memorial in Montgomery, Alabama, honors forty people who lost their lives during the struggle for equality between 1954 and 1968. This list includes civil rights workers as well as victims of antiblack violence.

Year	Deaths	Year	Deaths
1955	4	1964	8
1957	1	1965	6
1959	1	1966	4
1961	1	1967	2
1962	2	1968	4
1963	7		

Becoming an FBI Special Agent

Job Description:
An FBI investigator's primary job is to solve crimes. Agents interrogate witnesses, gather evidence from crime scenes, communicate with members of other law enforcement agencies, and stage raids on buildings suspected of harboring criminals or criminal activity. FBI officials frequently point out that there is really no such thing as a typical day for an FBI agent.

FBI agents section off a crime scene before beginning an investigation.

Education:
A four-year college degree is required. Courses of study in languages, law, and accounting are preferred.

Qualifications:
Candidates must pass drug tests and a vision exam and must demonstrate that they are in good physical condition. Applicants cannot have been convicted of a felony. There are strict age limits: Candidates for special agent training must be at least twenty-three and not more than thirty-six years old. Communication skills and the ability to work as part of a team are both essential. Applicants are also subjected to rigorous and lengthy background checks.

Additional Information:
Like other police work, being an FBI agent can be quite dangerous.

Salary:
Typically $40,000 to $75,000 per year. FBI investigators tend to be better paid than their counterparts in state and local police departments.

out against the "invasion" of the civil rights activists and expressed little willingness to support or protect the Freedom Summer workers. It seemed likely that no state or local law enforcement agency would spend much time or energy on an investigation.

The only alternative, therefore, was the federal government—specifically, the national police force known as the Federal Bureau of Investigation, or FBI. Friends of Chaney, Goodman, and Schwerner knew, however, that it would be difficult to get the help of this organization. In several earlier crimes against civil rights workers elsewhere in the South, the FBI had either been slow to become involved or declined to enter the case altogether. Part of the reason was J. Edgar Hoover, the FBI's longtime director, who was noted for his opposition to the goals of the civil rights movement. Part, too, was the prevailing FBI belief that civil rights workers called for federal support whenever they ventured into dangerous areas. Civil rights advocates, grumbled Hoover, "want us to be bodyguards and to give personal protection"[23]—but given the FBI's limited resources, Hoover argued, this level of support was not possible.

The structure of the American legal system also kept the FBI from investigating some of these earlier crimes. Most crimes violate only state laws, not the laws of the federal government. Even murder is seldom a federal offense. Investigation into these crimes, therefore, is primarily the responsibility of state and local governments. Although a 1960 law gave the FBI the authority to intervene in civil rights cases, Hoover had no desire to interfere with the long-standing tradition of allowing local agencies to solve crimes themselves.

Certainly, the FBI is sometimes brought in to work on a local case. This generally happens in one of two ways. Either local officials request federal assistance or FBI involvement is ordered by the federal Department of Justice—headed by the

By the Numbers

110

Estimated number of Ku Klux Klan chapters currently active in the United States

U.S. attorney general, who answers in turn to the president. In the years preceding 1964, however, southern police departments had not welcomed FBI involvement in civil rights cases. Nor had the two previous presidents, Dwight D. Eisenhower and John Kennedy, used their authority to order FBI involvement in civil rights investigations. For personal and political reasons, both Eisenhower and Kennedy instead had most often followed the wishes of southern governors, sheriffs, and state troopers, and not insisted that the FBI take part in these cases.

By 1964, however, the political climate had changed. The new president, Lyndon Johnson, was a much stronger supporter of civil rights than either Eisenhower or Kennedy. Together with U.S. attorney general Robert Kennedy—a brother of the former president and a solid civil rights advocate himself—Johnson had several times used federal authority to enforce civil rights legislation passed by the national government. Just two days before the disappearance of Chaney, Goodman, and Schwerner, in fact, Johnson had used his political muscle to push a new and much more powerful civil rights act through Congress. Heartened by this knowledge, the staffers at the community center hoped they might succeed in enlisting the help of the FBI in the search for the three missing men.

The FBI Becomes Involved

As word of the disappearance spread throughout the South, activists in Mississippi and elsewhere began calling any government official who might be able to help. Among these was senior Justice Department official John Doar, who had more experience with civil rights cases than most other members of his organization. Early on the morning of June 22, movement leaders in Atlanta reached Doar by telephone and told him what had happened. Appalled by the news and deeply concerned for the safety of the three missing men, Doar promised to do what he could. "I have invested the FBI with the power to look into this,"[24] he told an activist that morning.

The families and friends of Schwerner and Goodman, too, tried to involve the federal government. Unlike most civil rights activists at the time, Schwerner and Goodman were not only white but came from upper-middle-class backgrounds. Their families were well-off, well-educated, and most of all, well-connected. The parents of the two men quickly met with their congressional representatives, then with staffers in the attorney general's office, and finally with President Johnson himself. "He was wonderful," Goodman's mother, Carolyn, recalled years afterward. "He said he was going to do everything possible."[25]

Other white northerners agitated for action as well. When her husband disappeared, Rita Schwerner was in Ohio, working with the next wave of Freedom Summer volunteers. Knowing that many of these young men and women came from affluent, influential families, Rita asked them to contact their own representatives to urge FBI involvement. Many northern newspapers and television stations also covered the case, putting it into the public eye even hundreds of miles from where the three men had disappeared.

As it turned out, however, the extra pressure employed by white northerners was probably unnecessary. In fact, the Justice

Justice Department attorney John Doar (left, holding paper) spearheaded the FBI's investigation into the disappearance of the three civil rights workers.

U.S. attorney general Robert Kennedy (center, standing), shown here in 1964, recommended that the FBI investigate Ku Klux Klan activities in Mississippi even before the three civil rights workers disappeared.

Department was well aware of the situation in Mississippi. For several months, both Doar and Kennedy had been keeping close tabs on Ku Klux Klan activity in the state. Only weeks earlier, Kennedy had recommended that the FBI be ordered into the state to question "individuals who may be or have been involved in acts of terrorism" and in particular to investigate "the possible participation in such acts by law enforcement officials."[26] The disappearance of Schwerner, Chaney, and Goodman was the excuse these federal officials needed to act.

The day after Goodman, Chaney, and Schwerner vanished, FBI officials summoned agents from New Orleans, Memphis, and elsewhere and sent them to Neshoba County. Some of these agents began searching the area for signs of the missing men. Others spoke with members of the local law enforcement community and with the African Americans of Neshoba County. The FBI was on the scene; a federal investigation was under way.

First Discovery

The first important break in the case came on June 23, two days after Schwerner, Goodman, and Chaney had disappeared. That morning, FBI investigator John Proctor received a call from Lonnie Hardin, the supervisor of a Choctaw reservation near Philadelphia. Hardin said that several Choctaw had reported seeing a burning car near a town called Bogue Chitto. Arriving on the scene, Proctor discovered that fire had destroyed much of the car. Still, the license plate remained intact, and enough of the vehicle's frame remained to make a positive identification. It was the station wagon that Chaney, Goodman, and Schwerner had driven to Neshoba County just two days before.

The discovery of the ruined car was deeply discouraging news to those who cared about the missing men. True, it did not present conclusive proof that the men had been murdered. An FBI search of the nearby swampland turned up no bodies, nor was there any evidence that the men had burned along with their car. Still, the destruction of the car strongly suggested that the three activists had met with violence. "The phone rang," recalled Carolyn Goodman, Andrew's mother, "and [a government official] told us they'd found their car[,] and I screamed. I knew that if they'd found the car that something horrible had happened."[27]

The burned-out car in which the civil rights workers were last seen was located on June 23.

Searchers drag the Pearl River in Neshoba County looking for the bodies of the three missing civil rights workers.

Unsettling as it was, however, locating the car did lend urgency to the investigation. Acting on the assumption that the missing men were either dead or being held prisoner, FBI officials quickly stepped up their presence in and around Neshoba County. "Mr. Hoover opened an office in Jackson," recalled Doar many years later, "and put some very excellent FBI investigators in charge of that investigation. They were not only good, but there were a lot of them."[28] The agents immediately began to organize a search of Neshoba County, and President Johnson commanded hundreds of U.S. military personnel to join them. "I want all the marines out," Carolyn Goodman remembered Johnson telling her. "I want the army out. I want the navy. I want them to go through the marshes, to dredge the Pearl River [which flowed through the county]."[29] Within a day or two, Neshoba County was full of federal agents and members of the armed forces, combing the county for a sign of the missing men.

> **By the Numbers**
>
> # 8
> **Number of hours of digging before agents found the bodies of three murdered civil rights workers**

Suspicion

Technically, the FBI agents were supposed to share authority with Rainey and other law enforcement personnel from Mississippi. Nevertheless, from the time the car was discovered, it was clear that the FBI was not only taking control of the investigation, but keeping information from local officials. Several hours passed, for instance, before the FBI informed the state highway patrol that the car had been found, and FBI officials politely but firmly kept Rainey away from the station wagon once he reached the scene. Even Governor Johnson was not kept informed. "No one conferred with me,"[30] he complained when the president decided to order military personnel to aid in the search.

To some, the FBI's actions seemed arbitrary, even short-sighted. But there were good reasons for the bureau's behavior. First, federal agents quickly noticed that most local authorities were investigating halfheartedly at best. Even an Alabama newspaper reporter sympathetic to Mississippi's white majority agreed. "Few Mississippians, officials or otherwise, seem to be doing very much active searching,"[31] the reporter noted. Just as civil rights leaders had anticipated, the disappearance of the three men did not appear to rank as a high priority with local officials.

Moreover, even after the discovery of the burned-out station wagon, many local whites were quick to call the disappearance a hoax. These Neshoba residents insisted that Goodman, Schwerner, and Chaney were perfectly safe. "They just hid somewhere," theorized Cecil Price, "trying to get a lot of publicity out of it."[32] Civil rights officials vehemently denied that the three workers were merely trying to win sympathy for their cause or hoping to direct northern anger at the South.

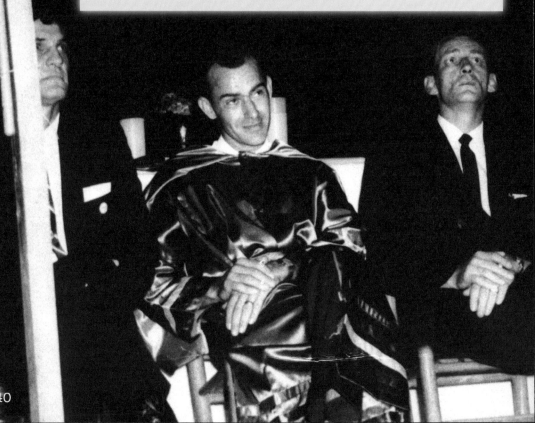

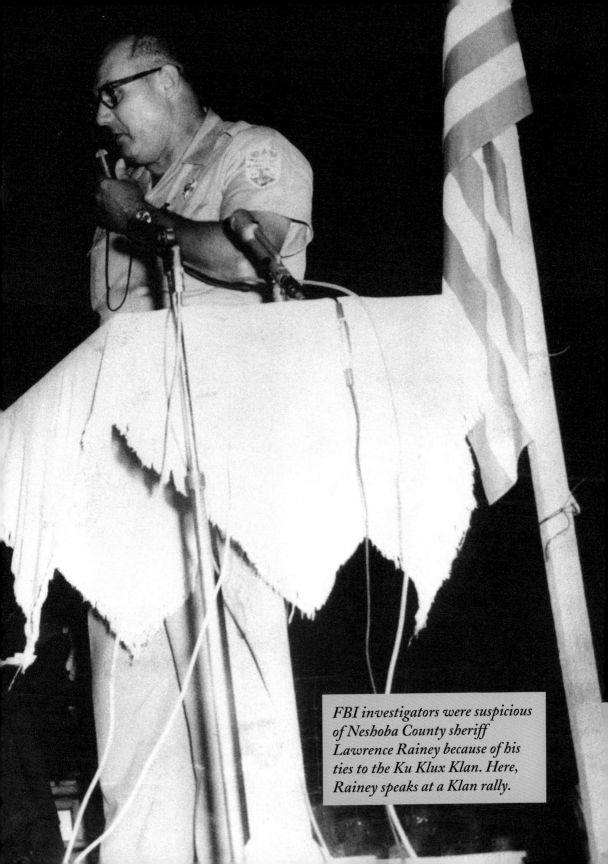

FBI investigators were suspicious of Neshoba County sheriff Lawrence Rainey because of his ties to the Ku Klux Klan. Here, Rainey speaks at a Klan rally.

Investigating a Disappearance

1 **Investigators first** determine that a person is actually missing.

2 **In the case of an adult,** it is usual to wait a certain period of time to see if the person reappears. (This delay may be waived if there is good reason to think that the missing person is in danger.)

3 **Investigators next** determine where, when, and by whom the person was last seen.

4 **At the same time,** investigators look into the missing person's background for possible clues to the disappearance. For example, they may check bank records to see if the missing person has been having financial problems.

5 **Forensic and eyewitness** evidence is used to try to determine where the person might have gone and (if applicable) with whom. Depending on the case, anything from bloodstains and torn scraps of clothing to airline records and credit card charges may help reveal the missing person's whereabouts.

Federal agents tended to agree. Certainly, they found it suspicious that so many of Mississippi's whites were unwilling to accept that the men might have met with violence.

Finally, early developments in the case raised puzzling questions about the doings of local law enforcement agents. According to Minnie Herring, the missing men had been released from the Philadelphia jail at six o'clock on the evening of June 21. Rainey agreed with Herring about the timing of the release; Price, however, now told federal investigators that the men had been set free after ten o'clock that night. Furthermore, Price told investigators that he had personally escorted the station wagon out of Philadelphia and part of the way to Meridian that night. The activists' car, however, had been found on the opposite side of the county.

Neither discrepancy was major. It was possible that Herring and Rainey simply had not been aware of the exact time when the men had been released. Likewise, the location of the car did not automatically imply that Price had lied about escorting the activists back toward Meridian. For reasons of their own, the men might have decided to turn around and drive to Bogue Chitto after Price had left them. And even if the men had indeed been attacked, there was no guarantee that Price had been involved. For all the FBI agents knew, someone unconnected to the sheriff's department had seized the men and forced them to drive across the county.

Nevertheless, federal agents could not bring themselves to ignore these discrepancies. Nor could they ignore Rainey's inflammatory remarks about civil rights activists, the reputed ties between him and the Ku Klux Klan, or his history of brutality against blacks. For all these reasons, federal agents distrusted Rainey and Price. And under the circumstances, it made sense to exclude them and their associates from the investigation as much as possible.

CHAPTER 3

The Discovery

Through the rest of June the search for the missing men continued. The work, most of it carried out under the Mississippi summer sun, was hot and grueling. The wildlife around Bogue Chitto made it dangerous as well. "Gripping heavy wooden clubs to fend off water moccasins and rattlesnakes," wrote one journalist, "400 sailors sludged through eastern Mississippi last week, poking and peering."[33] Navy helicopter pilots surveyed the countryside from the air as well, looking for clues to the men's fate.

Still, the combined efforts of the searchers turned up no sign of the three missing workers either in or around Bogue Chitto. Unwilling to give up, FBI officials directed the search to continue in other parts of the county. Military personnel dragged the county's rivers and lakes; divers from a naval base in South Carolina were assigned to explore the bottom of one bayou. Searchers also paid particular attention to the part of the highway where Price claimed he had last seen the three men. But through June and well into July, the searchers found nothing of any consequence.

By this time, most of the searchers were reasonably certain that the three missing men were dead. Still, federal officials vowed to keep looking until the bodies were found—and just as important, until those who had killed them had been brought to justice. "Instructions have been issued that no amount of material, manpower, or expense is to be spared,"[34] Hoover told President Johnson after returning from a brief trip to Mississippi in mid-July.

Investigators search a swampy area in Mississippi for clues to the disappearance of Goodman, Schwerner, and Chaney.

Privately, however, Hoover and other federal agents despaired of ever finding the bodies of Goodman, Schwerner, and Chaney in this manner. No matter how many men took part in the search, success was unlikely. Neshoba County was full of swamps, lakes, and isolated forests where it would be easy to hide three corpses. With little if any help from the people who knew the county best, it would take the searchers years to check all the possible hiding places. Though it was conceivable that the searchers would stumble upon the corpses at any given moment, the odds were strongly against them.

Fingerprints and Body Identification

While murder victims are often identified by their fingerprints, not all corpses have usable fingerprints. Fingerprints are a feature of the flesh rather than of the skeleton. Thus, once the flesh has begun to decompose, it is no longer possible to use fingerprints to identify a body. In the case of Goodman, Schwerner, and Chaney, just a few weeks in the dam had rotted the three bodies to the point where fingerprints were no longer present.

Instead of fingerprints, then, investigators used teeth to positively identify two of the three civil rights workers. Teeth are sturdy and almost as distinctive as fingerprints. Investigators obtained Schwerner's and Goodman's dental records (there were no dental records for Chaney) and compared the information in those charts with the teeth of the corpses. The gaps, overlaps, fillings, and missing teeth described in the dental records matched the teeth of the bodies. Later, investigators checked samples of hairs and skin taken from the three bodies against the medical records of the three men; these, too, matched. It was therefore not necessary to have perfect fingerprints in order to identify the three men beyond question.

As a result, the search was only one prong of a larger strategy. Even while searchers continued to slog through Neshoba County's rivers and forests, federal agents under the direction of the FBI's Joseph Sullivan fanned out across the county to conduct interviews with local residents. These interviews returned some useful information. For example, investigators soon were able to compile a list of probable Ku Klux Klan members in the area—a group that did indeed include both Rainey and Price along with a number of other local men, most of them lower middle class and poorly educated.

"The *Real* Search"

Obtaining this information, however, was difficult, time-consuming, and frustrating. Fearing reprisals from local whites, many blacks refused to speak to the investigators. Whites, in turn, did not seem to fear the FBI's power and investigative abilities. Instead, they used their interviews to debate civil rights issues with federal agents and to provide them with useless information. "We had a lot of jolly talks with Klansmen and wasted a lot of time," Sullivan said. "You can talk and talk to them and never get anywhere."[35]

To shake loose pertinent information, the FBI had one final strategy: bribery. Investigators knew that members of the Ku Klux Klan were extremely guarded about their activities when speaking to outsiders, but had few secrets where other Klansmen were concerned. If the three civil rights workers had been the victims of violence, investigators were reasonably certain that a dozen or more people in and around the county knew what had happened. If any of these citizens could be persuaded to talk, the entire case might be solved. Accordingly, FBI agents made it clear that they would handsomely reward any informer who could lead them to the three bodies. They also promised to keep the informant's identity a secret, thus forestalling revenge from others involved in the crime.

As many FBI agents saw it, the hunt for an informer was at the heart of the Neshoba County investigation. "We won't find anything," a federal official predicted, referring to the physical search for the three corpses. "But we have to keep dragging rivers and beating the bushes, while the *real* search goes on: the search for that citizen who, for protection and money, will eventually take us to the bodies."[36]

Hostility and Anger

However, as the investigation progressed, tempers on both sides began to fray. White southerners, in particular, became angry. Many Mississippians resented the attention the federal government was paying to the case. Governor Johnson, for instance, noted that people disappeared in places besides Mississippi, too. "It happens in New York every night,"[37] he observed pointedly—yet no one in the national government, Johnson complained, was suggesting that federal agents swarm across Manhattan the way they had entered Neshoba County.

Indeed, many southerners felt that Lyndon Johnson and the FBI were unfairly making an example of Mississippi. In their opinion, the federal government was committed to the success of the civil rights movement and the destruction of the southern way of life. A few believed that the nation's leaders were taking direct orders from such activists as Martin Luther King Jr. As a result, they charged, FBI agents were paying excessive attention to the disappearance of the three men. "Would there be such a hue and cry if anyone [other than civil rights workers] had disappeared?" asked a Meridian newspaper. "Of course not!"[38]

Some white Mississippians continued to propose as well that the missing men might not have met with violence. In late July, U.S. senator James Eastland repeated earlier assertions that Chaney, Schwerner, and Goodman might have staged their disappearance. "No one wants to charge that a hoax has been perpetrated," Eastland said. However, he added, as long as there was no actual evidence of a crime, "the people of America will be justified in considering other alternatives . . . instead of accepting as true the accusation of the agitators that [a] heinous crime has been committed."[39] Governor Johnson, in turn, suggested that the three men had fled to Cuba, a Communist country that was a bitter enemy of the United States. His comments reflected a widespread belief among white southerners that the civil rights movement was secretly aligned with Communist governments.

J. Edgar Hoover

For many years, J. Edgar Hoover's name was synonymous with the FBI. Born in 1895, Hoover earned a law degree in 1916 and began working for the Department of Justice the following year. In 1919 he became special assistant to the U.S. attorney general; five years later, not yet thirty, he became the director of the FBI, then known simply as the Bureau of Investigation. Hoover was a driving force behind the growth and effectiveness of the FBI. He improved training procedures for new recruits, greatly improved the FBI's ability to collect and use forensic evidence, established a fingerprint database, and opened crime labs designed to bring crime-solving into a more technological age. Hoover died in 1972 following a forty-eight-year career as head of the FBI.

J. Edgar Hoover led the FBI for nearly fifty years.

At the same time, some civil rights activists believed that the investigation was not progressing swiftly enough. Rita Schwerner was particularly angry. Early on, she complained that the search was only for show, that the FBI was not really interested in finding the men or their killers. When Deputy Attorney General Nicholas Katzenbach took issue with her statement, she charged that Katzenbach and other members of the administration had been "bought off . . . by southern politicians."[40] Other activists picketed the Justice Department, decrying the federal government's decision not to offer protection to individual civil rights workers.

Rita Schwerner, wife of Mickey Schwerner, complained about the slow pace of the investigation into her husband's disappearance.

The Bodies

Faced with hostility from both sides, Hoover and Sullivan simply continued their efforts. By the end of July, the FBI's promised reward for information had risen to $30,000, an enormous sum of money in 1964. The potential payoff finally swayed a Neshoba County resident whose name has never been officially revealed. On the last day of July, this informer contacted a Mississippi law enforcement official, one of the few openly assisting the FBI investigation, and said that he had the information the FBI was seeking. Specifically, he said, he knew exactly where the bodies were buried: in a large earth dam not far from where the three men had disappeared.

Officials excavate the site where the bodies of the civil rights workers were hidden.

FBI agents quickly located the dam, which was on an isolated piece of property owned by a Neshoba County man named Olen Burrage. The dam had been built only recently. It was huge—over 500 feet (153m) long and 20 feet (6m) high. Clearly, the dam was far too large to take apart with hand tools. Taking pains to keep their activities a secret from the sheriff's office, federal agents brought excavating equipment into the area. At the same time, they obtained a warrant to search Burrage's property. On August 4, they began digging into the dam.

Because of the size of the dam, the agents on the scene anticipated that the digging might last a week, even ten days. They were wrong. Less than three hours after cutting into the dam for the first time, agents noticed what a formal report later termed "the faint odor of decaying organic material."[41] The odor became stronger as they dug deeper. At three o'clock the diggers switched to hand tools. Minutes later, they scraped away the last pieces of earth—and revealed the distinct outlines of a human body. By five fifteen they had located two more. The informer, whoever he was, had been telling the truth.

Autopsies

Although the faces of the three men were badly decomposed, identification was not difficult. Schwerner's wallet was found in the pants pocket of the first corpse; Goodman's wallet was in a pocket of the second. The third corpse was that of a black man. The bodies were transported to Jackson, the state capital, where pathologists compared dental records, analyzed hair samples, and carried out other tests designed to establish the identity of the three bodies. The tests only verified what the investigators already knew: These were the corpses of Schwerner, Goodman, and Chaney.

The autopsies on the three bodies also revealed how the men had died. The bodies of Schwerner and Goodman each contained a single bullet, and traces of gunpowder indicated that they had been fired upon from close range. Chaney's body, in contrast, contained three bullets. Four of the five bullets had come from the same gun, but one of the bullets recovered from Chaney's body did not match the others. Evidently, two different guns had been used. This information did not tell investigators who had shot the three men, where they had been killed, or when they had died. Still, it was a start.

High Gear

The discovery of the bodies put to rest any serious speculation that the disappearance had been a hoax. Indeed, many white Mississippians were deeply shaken by the news that the men

Autopsies performed on the bodies of the civil rights workers revealed that all three had been shot.

had been murdered. Those who had firmly believed that Goodman, Schwerner, and Chaney had burned their own car and gone into hiding were shocked to discover that the men really had been killed. "I just didn't think we had people like that around,"[42] mused a Jackson resident.

Others, however, appeared more shaken by the presence of a willing informer in Neshoba County. The Ku Klux Klan was a secretive organization. Members pledged to reveal nothing about the group's activities to outsiders. Yet one Klansman had done exactly that. Many white Mississippians, even those without evident ties to the Klan, were surprised by the informant's breach of the organization's code of silence. A few were furious. As one Philadelphia resident angrily said to a reporter, "Somebody finally went and opened up."[43]

The FBI next turned its energies to the question of who had been responsible for the murders. Investigators knew

Law enforcement officials transport the body of one of the civil rights workers.

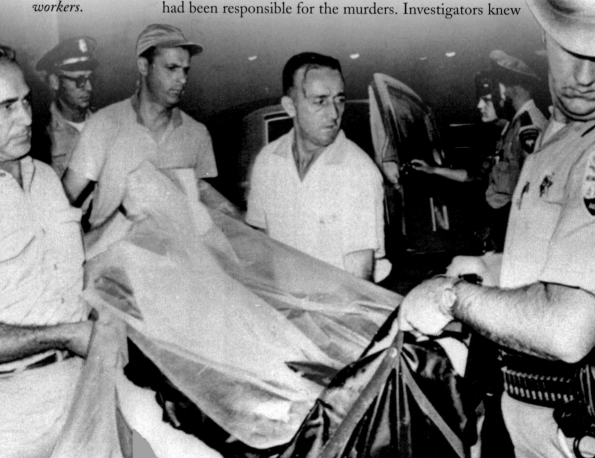

that the discovery of the bodies had caught local Klansmen off balance, and they made excellent use of that fact. Agents quickly sowed mistrust among local white supremacists, suggesting that first one Klan leader, then another, might have been the source of their earlier information. In interviews, they pretended to know more than they did, urging possible suspects to turn informer themselves before they were arrested based on information provided by another person involved in the plot.

The results were just what Sullivan and other agents had hoped. The arrogant confidence shown by Neshoba County's Klansmen earlier in the summer vanished, replaced by a palpable tension. The nervousness, in fact, extended as far as Meridian. One suspect, Doyle Barnette, moved abruptly to Louisiana when investigators started coming to his door. Another reputed Klansman, James Jordan, also left the area. Rainey, claiming that he was being excluded from FBI deliberations, stopped cooperating with federal investigators altogether.

The investigation continued. The FBI had suspected that the three men had been murdered; now, it had the bodies as proof. True, there was still no clear indication of what had happened the night that Goodman, Chaney, and Schwerner were killed. And though there were suspects in the murder, there was as yet no evidence to implicate any of them. Nonetheless, FBI agents were optimistic. Before long, they anticipated, they would break the case—and bring the killers of the three civil rights workers to justice.

CHAPTER 4

Confessions

By the end of the summer, the constant pressure applied by federal agents began to pay off. The next Klansman to break was a police officer named Wallace Miller, who held a leadership post in the Meridian Klan chapter. Though he had no direct involvement in the disappearance of the three civil rights workers, Miller had learned details about the killings from fellow Klansmen. Miller was not as virulent a racist as many other Klansmen, and he was disturbed to learn that the three missing men had been murdered. By mid-September, Miller's concerns had led him to tell the FBI what he knew—in exchange for a few thousand dollars and a promise of protection from the possible wrath of other Klan members.

Miller made it clear to investigators that all his information was secondhand. He had been neither at the crime scene itself, he said, nor active in planning the murders. Thus, he could not be sure who had actually killed Chaney, Schwerner, and Goodman. Nonetheless, Miller did single out two men as the chief planners of the crime. One, Sam Bowers, a businessman from the nearby community of Laurel, was an Imperial Wizard, or high-ranking official in charge of several Klan chapters in the region. The other was a Neshoba County man named Edgar Ray Killen, a sawmill operator and part-time preacher. Miller told investigators, in fact, that he had met with Killen a few days after the three civil rights activists had vanished. During the meeting, he explained, Killen had told Miller "that [the men] had been shot; that they were dead; and that they were buried in a dam about fifteen feet [4.6m] deep."[44]

Miller's information regarding Bowers and Killen was certainly valuable. It was his position as a Klan leader, however,

Police officer Wallace Miller implicated sawmill operator Edgar Ray Killen (top) and businessman Sam Bowers (bottom) in the killings.

Delmar Dennis, shown here displaying the hood he wore as a member of the Ku Klux Klan, cooperated with the FBI as an informer.

that made him most useful to federal investigators. Miller knew a great deal about how the organization operated. He told federal agents precisely how new members were recruited, how new officers were chosen, and how organizational decisions were made. All this information helped investigators immeasurably in trying to understand the workings of the local Klan chapters.

FBI agents instructed Miller to continue going to regular Klan meetings and taking part in ordinary Klan activities. They told him, however, to funnel to the FBI whatever new information he heard about the killings, future Klan projects, or changes in the organization's structure. Miller was soon joined in this role by another Meridian Klansman turned informer, a preacher named Delmar Dennis. As one historian put it, Dennis was "hot-wired right into the center"[45] of the local Klan organization. Personable and articulate, Dennis was a close confidant of Bowers. Between the two of them, Miller and Dennis kept the FBI abreast of the Klan's activities during the fall of 1964.

Unfortunately for the FBI, Dennis, like Miller, had not been present at the scene of the crime. Both men's knowledge of the murders consisted only of what other people had told them. Hoover, Doar, and Sullivan knew they could not hope to convict any Klansmen of murder without at least one eyewitness account of their involvement. Unless the investigators could find direct evidence implicating one or more of these Klansmen, then, all the work the FBI had done would be in vain.

Eyewitness Accounts

The attention of FBI agents soon focused on two men: James Jordan and Doyle Barnette. Both had been named as Klansmen by the informants Dennis and Miller; both had left the area soon after the discovery of the bodies. And Miller had told investigators that he believed Jordan, at least, to have been on the scene when the three men were killed. FBI officials saw Jordan and Barnette as possible weak links, at least in comparison to Killen, Price, Bowers, and others whose names had appeared repeatedly during the investigation. Accordingly, agents paid a series of visits to Jordan and Barnette, hoping to pressure them into revealing what they knew about the murders of Goodman, Schwerner, and Chaney.

Jordan was the first to be approached. Initially, he denied any knowledge of the crime. But FBI agent John Proctor warned Jordan that the bureau would soon have the information it sought, with or without Jordan's cooperation. Jordan's choice, as Proctor put it, was stark: "You either get on the right side," he told Jordan, "or you can go to jail."[46] Other investigators used similar tactics with Barnette when they visited him at his new home in Louisiana.

Slowly, the threats wore the two men down. By late October, Jordan finally agreed to tell FBI officials what he knew; Barnette followed suit a few weeks later. Both negotiated payment for their stories, and both, like Miller and Dennis, received the promise of protection from Klan retaliation. Their stories, though told separately, were similar—and chilling. At last, the FBI had the eyewitness accounts it needed.

The Plan

According to both Jordan and Barnette, the plan to kill the civil rights workers had been put together soon after the arrest of Schwerner, Chaney, and Goodman on speeding charges. Once the three men had been put in jail, Jordan and Barnette explained, Deputy Sheriff Price had called Killen, the preacher and sawmill operator from Neshoba County. Killen had quickly summoned several other Klansmen to a meeting; Jordan and Barnette were among those in attendance.

According to the two informers, Killen explained that three civil rights workers were soon to be released from the

Under pressure from the FBI, Klansman Doyle Barnette (left) agreed to reveal what he knew about the murders of the civil rights workers.

Philadelphia jail. As Jordan remembered it, Killen added that the three activists "needed their rear ends tore up."[47] The Klansmen present needed no further encouragement. They drove to the jail, turned off their engines, and waited for the three men to be released. They were soon joined by several other men from Meridian, who had also been alerted to the plan. By nine thirty, at least three cars filled with Klansmen were parked near the Philadelphia courthouse.

Neither Jordan nor Barnette was able to give a complete list of the men present. They did, however, agree that Killen, who had called the meeting and urged those attending to act, was not among them. Both in Mississippi and elsewhere, it was common practice for Klan leaders to avoid participating in any actual violence. Accordingly, some of the men dropped Killen off at a funeral in Philadelphia. Killen's presence at the funeral, they knew, would help him establish an alibi should a case ever come to trial.

Murder

When the three civil rights workers were released from jail, they began driving back to Meridian. According to both Jordan and Barnette, Price trailed them in his patrol car with a convoy of Klan members close behind. For a time, the Klansmen were content simply to follow. But near the Neshoba County line, they made their move. "Price pulled the station wagon over to the side of the road by turning on his red light," Jordan told investigators. "He told the three men to get out and get in his car."[48] Then, both Jordan and Barnette agreed, Price drove the three activists along the highway and into an isolated turnoff known as Rock Cut Road.

In his account, Jordan claimed that the other Klansmen left him to serve as a sentry at the intersection of Rock Cut Road and the highway. Thus, he insisted, he did not actually witness what came next. As Barnette told the story, though, Price led the entire group—including Jordan—about a mile up Rock Cut Road, then brought the procession to a halt. At this point, Wayne Roberts, a Klansman from Meridian who had been traveling in the last vehicle of the procession, ran to Price's car, threw open the rear door, and pulled Schwerner roughly from the vehicle. "Are you that nigger lover[?]"[49] Roberts demanded, waving a pistol at the young civil rights activist.

Schwerner's response was probably intended to be soothing. "Sir," he said, "I know just how you feel."[50] But Roberts was too irate to be calmed. According to Barnette, Roberts aimed his pistol at Schwerner and fired. Since Roberts was standing no more than a foot or two away from the activist, the shot could hardly have missed its intended target. Schwerner crumpled to the ground, dead. Roberts then seized Goodman, pulled him out onto the road, and killed him with a second bullet.

At this point, Barnette continued, James Jordan called out "Save one for me."[51] Roberts moved aside to allow Jordan to pull Chaney out of the car. "I remember Chaney backing up," Barnette told investigators, "facing the road . . . and Jordan stood in the middle of the road and shot him. I do not remember how many times Jordan shot." But Barnette did remember Jordan's words to Roberts after Chaney's death. "You didn't leave me anything but a nigger," Barnette quoted his fellow Klansman as complaining, "but at least I killed me a nigger."[52]

The story was not yet done. Jordan and Barnette, once again in agreement, now described the aftermath of the murders: how the Klansmen brought the bodies to Burrage's property; how they used a bulldozer to scoop out a hole some 14 feet (4m) below the surface of the dam; how other members of the group took the activists' station wagon to Bogue Chitto and burned it there. Barnette concluded his account by describing a meeting between him, Rainey, and several other Klansmen perhaps three hours after the three civil rights workers had been killed. "We talked for 2 or 3 minutes," he told investigators, "and then someone said that we better not talk about this and Sheriff Rainey said 'I'll kill anyone who talks, even if it was my own brother.'"[53]

Filing Charges

The accounts of Barnette and Jordan were not perfect. They contradicted each other in places, most notably over the question of Jordan's whereabouts and the question of who had killed Chaney. Neither Barnette nor Jordan could name all the Klan members on the scene. Neither had been involved in the plotting from the very beginning. And as Barnette and Jordan told the story, it was clear that some men deeply involved in the conspiracy, such as Cecil Price and Edgar Ray Killen, either had not been present at Rock Cut Road or had not actually killed any of the three men themselves.

Fortunately for the investigators, the definition of murder was rather broad. Under the law, it was possible to be found guilty of murder without physically killing another person. Anyone who simply helped to carry out a killing was subject to murder charges. Thus, Barnette's account incriminated not just the two shooters, Roberts and Jordan, but all the other

Klansmen who had been present at Rock Cut Road as well. Even Killen and Bowers, who according to Jordan and Barnette had organized the crime, could be charged with murder under the law.

There was one serious difficulty, however. As Justice Department officials were well aware, murder was a state crime. To convict the Klansmen of murder, the case would have to be argued by Mississippi officials in a Mississippi state court. Unfortunately for the investigators, the state seemed uninterested in bringing murder charges in the case of the three murdered men. Mississippi law enforcement officials, after all, had been reluctant to investigate the case from the start. And even after the confessions of Barnette and Jordan, Governor Johnson advised against pursuing murder charges. The case against the Klansmen was extremely weak, he argued. A murder trial, he said, "would be laughed out of the country."[54]

Witness Doyle Barnette identified Wayne Roberts (pictured) as the person who shot Goodman and Schwerner to death.

Conspiracy

Investigators who hoped for murder charges faced another obstacle, too. The state judge who presided over murder cases in that part of Mississippi, O.A. Barnett, was not only a staunch segregationist, but also a distant relative of some of the possible defendants. Federal officials hoped that Barnett would step aside because of his family connections and pass the case on to another judge. They doubted, however, that he would. On the contrary, they expected Barnett to prejudge the case, allow fervent white supremacists to serve on the jury, and make sure to rule in favor of the men who had been charged with the crime.

In the end, FBI agents decided not to push for a charge of murder. Instead, they fell back on a little-known and seldom-used law passed in 1870. This law made it a crime

Viola Liuzzo

Viola Liuzzo was a white woman from Detroit who traveled to Alabama to work for civil rights. In March 1965, while shuttling black civil rights activists between Selma and Montgomery, Liuzzo was shot from a passing car and killed. Doubtful that they could win a murder conviction in Alabama, FBI officials arrested the people they believed had shot Liuzzo and charged them with conspiracy—just as they had the Klansmen suspected of killing Goodman, Chaney, and Schwerner. The Liuzzo trial moved along much more quickly than the Freedom Summer killings in Mississippi. In December 1965, Liuzzo's murderers were convicted of conspiracy and given the maximum ten-year sentences. The Liuzzo prosecution afforded government attorneys excellent practice in bringing conspiracy charges, helping them establish a strong case against the killers of the three civil rights workers in Mississippi.

Alabama state troopers stand guard over the car of slain housewife and civil rights activist Viola Liuzzo (left).

for two or more people to "conspire to injure, oppress, threaten, or intimidate any citizen in the free exercise or enjoyment of any right or privilege secured to him by the Constitution or laws of the United States."[55] In essence, the law was an anticonspiracy statute designed to protect the civil and constitutional rights of Americans when state laws failed to do so.

Officials in the Justice Department were fully aware that a charge of conspiracy was a poor substitute for a charge of murder. Certainly Chaney, Goodman, and Schwerner had suffered far more than a mere deprivation of civil rights. The crime of conspiracy, moreover, was not nearly as serious as murder. Those convicted could be fined no more than five thousand dollars and given a prison sentence that could not exceed ten years. Nor was it certain that the men would be found guilty even if federal charges were filed. Since the conspiracy involved a Mississippi case, any trials would be held in Mississippi—with a jury probably made up of people unsympathetic to the civil rights movement.

But Justice Department officials decided that they had no choice. In their opinion, there was a chance that a Mississippi jury might convict the Klansmen of the relatively mild charge of conspiracy. There was no chance at all, they believed, that a jury would convict the men of murder, if the case ever came to trial to begin with. A guilty verdict on a conspiracy charge was better than an acquittal on a charge of murder. As federal officials saw it, then, the conspiracy charge represented the only hope of bringing the killers of Goodman, Chaney, and Schwerner to justice.

CHAPTER 5

The Trial

On the morning of December 4, 1964, federal agents arrested nineteen men on conspiracy charges in connection with the case. In the official language of the indictment, these men stood accused of plotting to "threaten, assault, shoot and kill"[56] Goodman, Schwerner, and Chaney. Two more men, who appeared to be minor players in the case, were charged with knowing about the conspiracy and failing to report it, a less serious charge. Thus, twenty-one people in all were arrested for the deaths of the three civil rights workers.

The twenty-one men had different levels of involvement in the killings. Working from what their informants had told them, FBI agents had decided that ten of the men had been present when the three civil rights workers died. This group included Wayne Roberts, who according to Barnette had fired the shots that killed Schwerner and Goodman, and Cecil Price, placed at the scene of the crime by the accounts of both Barnette and Jordan. All ten were taken into custody, including Jordan and Barnette; their agreements with the FBI did not shield them from prosecution.

The other eleven arrested, however, had not been at Rock Cut Road when Schwerner, Chaney, and Goodman died. Among these men were Burrage, who owned the dam inside which the three corpses had been concealed, and Herman Tucker, who according to both Jordan and Barnette had operated the bulldozer used to bury the bodies that night. This group also included Rainey, who by all accounts had been nowhere near the scene of the crime, and Killen, who had been at a funeral home when the crime had allegedly been committed. Like the charge of murder, the charge of conspiracy

Although many Southern whites were angered at the arrests of nineteen men in connection with the murders, African American leaders such as Martin Luther King Jr. praised the FBI for its work.

MICHAEL HENRY SCHWERNER

JAMES EARL CHANEY

ANDREW GOODMAN

did not require that all the men were present when the killings were carried out—merely that those arrested knew about the crime and were involved in its commission.

Federal agents did not expect the men to remain in custody for long, and indeed they did not. The men quickly appeared before U.S. commissioner Esther Carter, a low-level judge. Defense attorneys told Carter that the men were solid citizens who were unlikely to run away before they could be tried. The lawyers suggested that their clients be released on bond—payment made to the court as a guarantee that a defendant will return for court appearances as scheduled. Agreeing with the defense attorneys, Carter set bond at five thousand dollars, which the men quickly paid. Free for the time being, they promised to return to Carter's court the following week for a preliminary hearing.

Civil rights advocates hailed the arrests. "I must commend the Federal Bureau of Investigation," said Martin Luther King Jr. "for the work they have done. . . . It renews my faith in democracy."[57] But many white Mississippians were appalled. Some charged that King and other civil rights leaders had agitated for the arrests—proof, in their eyes, that the FBI and the Justice Department were under the thumb of the activists. And there was widespread support for the defendants and their segregationist stand. "It took me an hour to get to work this morning," Price told a reporter a day or two after his arrest. "I had to shake so many hands."[58]

Carter's Ruling

The preliminary hearing took place on December 10 in Carter's Meridian courtroom. The purpose of the hearing was simply to determine if prosecutors had a reasonable case against the twenty-one men. At such hearings, the commissioner would typically hear a broad outline of the evidence against the defendants and then agree that there was reason to believe that they might be guilty. The case would then go forward. Occasionally, a commissioner might rule against the prosecution, thus requiring that the charges against the defendants be dropped, but Justice Department officials believed that their evidence was too strong for Carter to act in that way.

The first witness in the preliminary hearing was Henry Rask, the FBI agent who had obtained a signed confession from Barnette. Barnette was now living in Louisiana, so he was not present in the courtroom. Moreover, Barnette's status as an informer made it advisable to keep him well away from his fellow Klansmen. Thus, the prosecution hoped to have Rask present Barnette's confession to the court. It was a common strategy, frequently used in preliminary hearings of this type, and prosecutors anticipated no difficulties.

Sheriff Lawrence Rainey, right, and deputy Cecil Price, left, laugh with a friend as they leave their preliminary hearing on December 10, 1964.

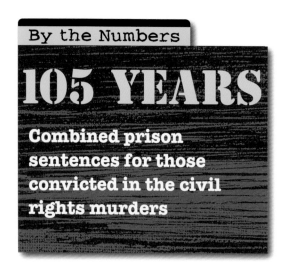

But Carter refused to allow Rask to speak. She insisted that Rask had no standing to discuss Barnette's confession. Coming from Rask, she said, the testimony would be hearsay—that is, based only on what he had been told by someone else. "I don't think it would be admissible,"[59] she concluded. Startled, Justice Department officials pointed out that it was common for investigators to present confessions in preliminary hearings of this sort. The lead prosecutor, Robert Owen, carefully explained that the Supreme Court had ruled this type of evidence to be admissible. Nonetheless, Carter held firm: She would not allow Rask's testimony.

The prosecutors knew that this was a fatal blow to their case. Without Rask's testimony, it was not possible to introduce Barnette's confession into the hearing. Without Barnette's confession, it seemed unlikely that Carter would find the government's arguments reasonable. Rather than do further battle with the commissioner, Justice Department officials decided instead to retrench. Temporarily dropping all charges against the twenty-one men, government lawyers decided to bypass Carter altogether. Instead, they pursued an indictment through another court, this one in Jackson.

First Steps

In January 1965, the case came before a federal grand jury—a panel convened by power of the national government but made up of ordinary residents of Jackson. After hearing a rough outline of the prosecution's case, the grand jury decided that the conspiracy charges were logical. The grand jury's decision did not in any way represent a conviction, nor did it even suggest that the men would eventually be found guilty. It did, however, allow the case to move forward and into the court of a federal judge named William Cox.

The prosecutors' triumph, however, was short-lived. In late February, Cox ruled that the anticonspiracy statute could be applied only to law enforcement officials in this case, not to ordinary citizens. Accordingly, he threw out the charges against all the defendants except Rainey, Price, and one Philadelphia police officer, and he sharply reduced the charges against these three men. Cox defended his decision on the grounds that the central issue in the case involved murder, a state crime, not the deprivation of civil rights. What had happened to Chaney, Schwerner, and Goodman, Cox argued, was absolutely "a heinous crime against Mississippi." But it was not, he insisted, "a crime against the United States."[60]

Cox had a long history of racism and hostility toward civil rights—he had once described a group of black activists as "a bunch of chimpanzees"[61]—so his ruling came as no surprise to prosecutors. Justice Department officials appealed his decision, hoping that a higher court would overturn Cox's ruling. Within a year, to the prosecution's delight, the U.S. Supreme Court voted unanimously against Cox. The conspiracy law did indeed apply to all defendants, the justices decided. The original charges stood; the trial could go forward. After a few further legal maneuvers, the trial finally began on October 7, 1967—more than three years after the murders.

"We Are Going to Try This Case"

The long delay had led to some changes in the prosecution's plan. Deciding that they should focus their resources on the men most likely to be convicted, government lawyers dropped the charges against five conspirators who, they felt, had been only peripherally involved in the plot. Acting on new information, they also added the names of three others—including Klan leader Bowers, named by Miller as one of the masterminds of the killings. The defendants now numbered nineteen, including Bowers, Killen, Price, Rainey, and Roberts.

Becoming a Federal Judge

Job Description:
A federal judge hears civil and criminal cases that are brought in federal courts. He or she may make rulings in the cases or may preside over the trial while a jury hears the evidence and gives the verdict. Judges are also responsible for sentencing defendants who are found guilty.

Before being appointed to the Supreme Court, Anthony Kennedy served as a federal judge.

Education and Qualifications:
According to the U.S. Constitution, there are no specific qualifications for becoming a federal judge. In practice, though, judges are expected to have strong legal backgrounds, including a degree from an accredited law school. When a vacancy occurs, the president nominates a candidate to fill the position. These prospective judges are either approved or rejected by the U.S. Senate. There is no specific checklist of qualifications that determines whether a particular candidate is accepted or turned down.

Additional Information:
Federal judges serve for life or until they choose to retire. There are three main levels of federal judges. The most important and powerful are the nine justices of the U.S. Supreme Court. Ranking below them are judges who serve on the various U.S. courts of appeals. The lowest level consists of U.S. district court judges. There are more than 850 federal judges in the United States; most of them serve at the district court level.

Salary:
$140,000–$200,000

The prosecutors were hopeful that justice might at last be done. Realistically, however, they believed that the odds were against them. Cox was still in charge of the case, after all, and most Justice Department officials thought that he would find yet another way to throw the case out of court. Some observers felt that Cox had shown bias even before the trial's opening arguments. In particular, though his original pool of jurors had included nineteen African Americans, he had allowed defense attorneys to eliminate every single black person on the list. The result was an all-white jury, which prosecutors felt would be unsympathetic to the government's case.

To the prosecutors' surprise, however, Cox opened the trial with a sharp rebuke to the defense. Immediately after the proceedings began, attorneys for the defendants badgered Cox to permit yet another delay. This time, Cox refused. "We are going to try this case," he told defense lawyers, "we are going to stay on it, we are going to stick to it, and we are going to get rid of it."[62] Cox's strong words and clear message impressed Justice Department officials and gave them hope that a fair trial might be possible.

A Turning Point

Their hopes were raised again by an event that took place later the same day. One of the first witnesses for the prosecution was Charles Johnson, a black preacher from Meridian who had worked closely with Schwerner. Lead prosecutor Doar used Johnson to establish why Schwerner had come to Mississippi and what he hoped to accomplish there. Under Doar's questioning, Johnson described the voter registration drives he and Schwerner had organized, Schwerner's commitment to economic justice, and Schwerner's deep concerns about police treatment of African Americans in Mississippi.

It was then defense attorney Laurel Weir's turn to question Johnson. Weir tried to discredit Schwerner by painting him as a dangerous revolutionary who hated all that America stood for. Weir asked Johnson whether Schwerner was an atheist, for instance, and what position Schwerner took on the Vietnam War, opposed at the time by many young whites who shared Schwerner's views on civil rights. Then Weir dropped a bombshell. "Isn't it true," he asked Johnson, "that you and Mr. Schwerner undertook to get young male Negroes to sign a statement that they would rape a white woman every week in the hot summer of 1964?"[63]

Johnson immediately denied the charge, but the question appalled Cox. He demanded to know why Weir would touch on such an offensive and inflammatory subject. When he discovered that the question had actually been written by Killen, Cox was even more outraged. "I'm not going to allow a farce to be made of this trial," he said. "I don't understand such a question as that, and I don't appreciate it. . . . I'm surprised at a question like that coming from a preacher, too."[64] Later, Doar saw the moment as a turning point. By reacting as he did, Doar said, "Cox made it clear he was taking the trial seriously. That made the jurors stop and think, 'If Judge Cox is taking this stand, we'd better meet our responsibility as well.'"[65]

The Verdict

The trial lasted over a week. Doar and his assistants called a number of witnesses to the stand in support of the government's case. Miller and Dennis told the jury about the workings of the local Klan chapters. Ernest Kirkland, who had accompanied the three civil rights workers to the ruins of Mount Zion Church, testified about the activists' movements on the day they died. Barnette refused to testify in person, but Jordan gave his account of what had happened to the three men. "This was a calculated, cold-blooded plot,"[66] Doar argued, summing up the government's case. He urged the jury to find all the defendants guilty of conspiracy as charged.

The defense attorneys did their best to counter the prosecution. Friends and relatives argued that the defendants were good, honorable citizens. Bowers, said one witness, was "a devoted Baptist, a man who has had an experience with the Lord."[67]

Justice Department attorney John Doar was the lead prosecutor in the 1967 trial of nineteen men charged with conspiracy in the murders of the three civil rights workers.

Edgar Ray Killen smiles as he enters the courthouse during his 1967 trial on conspiracy charges.

Defense lawyers questioned the truthfulness of Jordan, Dennis, and Miller, noting that the informers had been paid for their testimony. Finally, they argued that the three civil rights workers had brought their deaths upon themselves. As one attorney put it, "Mississippians rightfully resent some hairy beatnik from another state visiting our state with hate and defying our people."[68]

With testimony and closing arguments complete, the case went to the jury on October 18. The following day, though, the jurors informed Cox that they could not agree on a verdict. Some members of the jury, they explained, wanted to acquit; others were ready to find at least some of the defendants guilty. There seemed to be no middle ground. The jurors asked that they be dismissed and requested that the trial begin again, this time with a different jury. Cox, however, refused. Citing the time and expense of the case thus far, Cox ordered the jurors to do their best to break the deadlock.

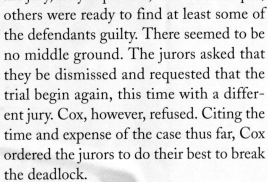

On October 20, one day after Cox's order to reach a verdict, the jury managed to do exactly that. Returning to the courtroom, the jurors announced that they had found seven of the defendants guilty as charged, among them Cecil Price, Wayne Roberts, Sam Bowers, and Doyle Barnette. Each of these seven men was sentenced to prison for his role in the conspiracy. Barnette and two others received a three-year sentence; Cox gave Bowers and Roberts the maximum penalty of ten years apiece. (Jordan, tried by a different jury in Atlanta, was later found guilty as well and sentenced to four years in prison.)

Acquittals

Despite their willingness to find these seven defendants guilty of conspiracy, however, the jury did not convict all who had been accused. The jurors acquitted eight of the defendants, including Sheriff Rainey, bulldozer operator Herman Tucker, and dam owner Olen Burrage. Moreover, members of the jury told Cox that they were still unable to agree on the guilt or innocence of the three remaining defendants, a group that included Killen. This time, Cox accepted the jury's inability to reach a decision. The law provided that these three men be released, so Killen walked out of the courtroom a free man.

Although they would have preferred to see all the defendants behind bars, Justice Department officials were delighted by the verdict. It had been a long, hard road, but the dogged, patient work of investigators and prosecutors alike had paid off. No previous Mississippi jury had ever convicted a white person of a crime against African Americans or civil rights workers. Despite the all-white jury, despite Cox's record of hostility to civil rights, despite Mississippi's long history of racism and segregation, justice had been done: limited and imperfect justice, to be sure, but justice nevertheless.

Justice Delayed

The Freedom Summer verdicts were a surprise, both within Mississippi and outside it. Still, there was general support for the outcome of the trial. Northerners, in particular, hoped that the guilty verdicts signaled a growing willingness on the part of white southerners to accept civil rights. The *New York Times*, for instance, wrote hopefully that the decision represented "the quiet revolution that is taking place in Southern attitudes"[69] involving race and segregation.

Among southerners, some staunch segregationists continued to argue that the defendants had been unfairly convicted. One supporter referred to them as "patriotic, white, Christian soldiers" who had fallen victim to a "Federal Court of injustice."[70] Still, plenty of whites across the South, even in Mississippi, applauded the ruling. Not everyone who opposed civil rights believed that murder was an appropriate response to the activism of Goodman, Schwerner, and Chaney. And those who did support at least the ideals of integration agreed with the *Times* that the verdict was a step in the right direction. The *Tupelo Journal*, a newspaper in northern Mississippi, even described the conviction of the seven men as "a turning point in race relations."[71]

The *Times* and the *Journal* were in fact correct. Over the ensuing years, Mississippi gradually became more open to new ideas about race. Segregationists slowly lost their grip on the culture and government of the state, and the features that made Mississippi distinctive—and dangerous to civil rights activity—began to fade. Household incomes for both blacks and whites rose; infant mortality fell. Blacks registered to vote; some held elective office as well. Integration of restaurants, hotels, and other facilities became a reality. In 1970, just three years after the close of the trial, Neshoba County not only desegregated its school system, but did so with very little controversy.

Reopening the Case

To some observers, Mississippi's progress suggested an opportunity to correct an earlier wrong. As the state's government and culture became less racially biased, more and more people urged that the state arrest the surviving conspirators and charge them with their real crime: murder. To do so, these advocates argued, would remove some of the shame caused by the state's earlier inaction. It would also ensure, at last, true justice.

Despite the political and social changes in the state, however, advocates of a new trial made little headway at first.

Important Dates of the Freedom Summer Killings

January 1964

James Chaney and Michael Schwerner meet in Meridian, Mississippi.

February–June

Chaney and Schwerner make more than thirty trips to Neshoba County to encourage others to join the fight for civil rights.

June 21

Andrew Goodman joins Chaney and Schwerner to question Mt. Zion Church members who had been beaten and interrogated by men who opposed the civil rights movement. The three activists disappear that afternoon.

June 23

Cheney, Schwerner, and Goodman's burned car is found near the town of Bogue Chitto.

Through the 1970s and 1980s, very few elected officials in Mississippi showed any interest in reopening the case. Most indicated an eagerness to put the events of the early 1960s behind them. U.S. senator Trent Lott spoke for many in 1989 when he strongly opposed the notion of filing new charges against the remaining conspirators. While he was certainly aware of the tragedy that had taken place in 1964, Lott explained, he simply "prefer[red] to focus on the progress Mississippi has made"[72] and feared that reviewing the case might cause people to lose sight of the positive steps his state had taken.

Within a decade, however, the situation began to change. In 1998, Bowers, the Klan leader who had received the maximum ten-year penalty for his role in the Freedom Summer killings, told an interviewer that the real mastermind of the

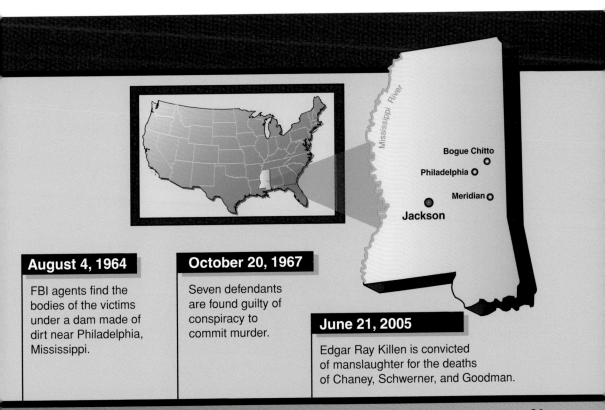

August 4, 1964

FBI agents find the bodies of the victims under a dam made of dirt near Philadelphia, Mississippi.

October 20, 1967

Seven defendants are found guilty of conspiracy to commit murder.

June 21, 2005

Edgar Ray Killen is convicted of manslaughter for the deaths of Chaney, Schwerner, and Goodman.

Mississippi River

Bogue Chitto

Philadelphia

Meridian

Jackson

murders had never been punished in any way. "I was quite delighted to be convicted," Bowers crowed, "and have the main instigator of the entire affair walk out of the courtroom a free man."[73] Though Bowers named no names, it was evident that he was referring to Edgar Ray Killen.

In 1999, largely in response to Bowers's words, state attorney general Mike Moore announced that he would reopen the case. Over the next few years, the state focused on determining whether it had a chance to convict Killen or any of the other original defendants. In the meantime, pressure on Mississippi officials to file murder charges increased. James Prince, the publisher of a Neshoba County newspaper, lobbied state officials to indict the surviving defendants. Despite advancing age, Carolyn Goodman, Andrew's mother, traveled from New York to Mississippi to do the same. In 2005, Moore's successor, Jim Hood, decided there was enough evidence against Killen to make new charges worth pursuing. A grand jury agreed. Killen was charged with three counts of murder.

As Bowers had noted, Killen had escaped penalty during the 1967 conspiracy trial; the jury had been unable to determine his guilt or innocence. In 2000, through interviews with some of the jurors who had served in the 1967 trial, Jackson journalist Jerry Mitchell learned what had actually happened during the jury's deliberations at the trial. In the case of Killen, the panel had voted 11–1 in favor of conviction. The one holdout said she simply could not bring herself to convict a preacher. Killen's part-time job had saved him from a guilty verdict and a prison sentence. Now, though, he was coming back to court.

A New Trial

Nearly forty years had passed since the original trial. Killen was approaching eighty and increasingly feeble. In his opinions about segregation and civil rights, however, he remained essentially unchanged. In 1999, for instance, he told a newspaper reporter that he approved of the 1968 assassination of

Clad in a bulletproof vest, Edgar Ray Killen is escorted into court in January 2005 for his arraignment on murder charges.

Mississippi attorney general Jim Hood, left, and Neshoba County prosecutor Mark Duncan, right, speak to members of the press after the sentencing of Edgar Ray Killen.

civil rights leader Martin Luther King Jr. That same year, he told another reporter that Schwerner, Chaney, and Goodman had been Communists and enemies of the United States. Nonetheless, he continued to maintain that he had not been involved in their deaths. "I'm sorry they got themselves killed," he said at the time. "But I can't show remorse for something I didn't do."[74]

Hood and Neshoba County district attorney Mark Duncan began the prosecution's case by calling several witnesses. One was Michael Schwerner's widow, Rita; another was Fannie Lee Chaney, James Chaney's eighty-two-year-old mother. Both

gave emotional testimony designed to make the dead men real to the jurors. Fannie Lee Chaney, for example, told the jury that James's younger brother Ben had wanted to go to Philadelphia with James the day the three men disappeared, but that she had kept Ben at home. "I told him to go on and go to Sunday school and he could be with him when [James] came back," she recalled. "But he never came back."[75]

To establish the murder charges, though, prosecutors had to prove that Killen had planned and ordered the murders. That meant providing the jury with eyewitness accounts. But many of the original conspirators were dead, and the rest had refused to testify against Killen—even in exchange for immunity from future prosecution. Accordingly, prosecutors read from testimony given originally at the 1967 conspiracy trial. Defense attorneys fought to exclude these accounts, noting that several witnesses in the original trial were now dead and could no longer be questioned about their statements, but Judge Marcus Gordon ruled that the testimony should stand.

Defense attorneys did their best to portray Killen as an innocent bystander. While admitting that their client had been an active Klansman for a time, they described him as a low-level functionary, not a leader. In any case, as one member of Killen's defense team told the jury, "You can't find this man

The Appeal Process

1. **A judge** in a lower court makes a ruling.

2. **The losing side appeals**—that is, argues that the judge has made a legal error. Not all rulings are subject to appeal.

3. **A judge** in a higher court hears the appeal and decides whether it has merit.

4. **If the judge** rules that the appeal is valid, the earlier decision is overturned. If not, the appeal may continue to the next higher court.

guilty just because he belonged to an organization of hate."[76] Finally, Killen's lawyers pointed to their elderly, frail client—who attended the trial in a wheelchair—and questioned what purpose would be served by putting such an old man into prison.

This last argument was a potentially powerful one. It was difficult to imagine Killen doing any further harm, and Duncan and Hood feared that jurors might set Killen free out of sympathy. In their summation to the jury, Duncan and Hood addressed this concern directly. The goal, they argued, was justice—justice for the families of the victims, justice for the

Mickey Schwerner's widow, Rita Schwerner Bender, and James Chaney's siblings, Ben Chaney and Barbara Chaney Dailey, attend the trial of Edgar Ray Killen .

victims themselves, and justice for the entire state of Mississippi. It was unconscionable, Duncan told the jury, to acquit Killen on the charges. "You can either change the history Edgar Ray Killen and the Klan wrote for us," Duncan argued, "or you [can] confirm it."[77]

"Three Lives"

On June 21, 2005, forty-one years to the day after Goodman, Schwerner, and Chaney were killed, the jury reached a verdict. Though unwilling to convict Killen of murder, they nonetheless convicted him on the lesser charge of manslaughter. Judge Gordon sentenced Killen to three twenty-year terms in prison, one for each of the victims. Under the law, it was the stiffest possible sentence he could give. Gordon said he knew that Killen had essentially no chance of living another sixty years. Still, he felt that the penalty was just. "There were three lives involved in this case," he said, "and the three lives should be recognized and treated equally."[78]

The verdict did not represent a complete end to the Freedom Summer murder case. Killen's lawyers immediately appealed the verdict, arguing once again that testimony from the 1967 case should not have been admitted into evidence. Some of Killen's supporters, including his brother, and some of his bitterest enemies, such as James Chaney's brother Ben, believe that other surviving conspirators should have been tried as well; Mississippi officials are leaving the case open, though most observers doubt that more charges will be filed. And, to be sure, not everyone approved of the verdict. Friends of Killen were outraged that the jury did not acquit him altogether, while Rita Schwerner, among others, expressed deep disappointment that Killen was not found guilty of murder.

Nonetheless, most observers found the verdict fair—and necessary. In 1967, federal prosecutors had done the best they could to avenge the three murdered civil rights activists. Working against a backdrop of fear and hatred, they had been successful, but only to a point. Now, changing conditions had

This marker stands today in Philadelphia, Mississippi, and memorializes James Chaney, Andrew Goodman, and Mickey Schwerner.

FREEDOM SUMMER MURDERS

On June 21, 1964, voting rights activists James Chaney, Andrew Goodman, and Michael Schwerner, who had come here to investigate the burning of Mt. Zion Church, were murdered. Victims of a Klan conspiracy, their deaths provoked national outrage and led to the first successful federal prosecution of a civil rights case in Mississippi.

MISSISSIPPI DEPARTMENT OF ARCHIVES AND HISTORY, 1989

Donated by the listeners of WKXI, Jackson, MS

made it possible to hold at least one man fully responsible for the deaths of Andrew Goodman, Mickey Schwerner, and James Chaney. In the process, the verdict and the sentence had helped Mississippi and all America begin to heal some old wounds. "It took a long, long time to win justice," remarked a Mississippi man shortly after the Killen verdict was announced. "But justice arrived last week. We can all rest and know that Mississippi and the whole South is now truly a part of this nation."[79]

Notes

Introduction: Freedom Summer 1964

1. Quoted in Henry Hampton and Steve Fayer, *Voices of Freedom*. New York: Bantam Books, 1990, p. xxvii.

2. Quoted in Hampton and Fayer, *Voices of Freedom*, p. xxiv.

3. Quoted in Susie Erenrich, ed., *Freedom Is a Constant Struggle*. Montgomery, AL: Black Belt Press, 1999, p. 91.

4. Quoted in Hampton and Fayer, *Voices of Freedom*, p. 123.

5. Ben Chaney, "The Struggle for Justice," *Human Rights*, Spring 2000, p. 3+.

6. Quoted in *Newsweek*, "The Invaders," June 29, 1964, p. 25.

7. Quoted in *Newsweek*, "The Invaders," p. 25.

8. Quoted in Hampton and Fayer, *Voices of Freedom*, p. 188.

9. Quoted in Doug McAdam, *Freedom Summer*. New York: Oxford University Press, 1988, p. 28.

Chapter One: The Disappearance

10. Quoted in Seth Cagin and Philip Dray, *We Are Not Afraid*. New York: Macmillan, 1988, p. 259.

11. Quoted in William Bradford Huie, *Three Lives for Mississippi*, rev. ed. New York: Signet, 1968, p. 59.

12. Quoted in Cagin and Dray, *We Are Not Afraid*, p. 271.

13. Quoted in *Mississippi Black Paper*. New York: Random House, 1965, p. 59.

14. Quoted in *Mississippi Black Paper*, p. 61.

15. Quoted in Huie, *Three Lives for Mississippi*, p. 75.

16. Quoted in Mary Winstead, *Back to Mississippi*. New York: Hyperion, 2002, p. 213.

17. Quoted in Huie, *Three Lives for Mississippi*, p. 73.

18. Quoted in Cagin and Dray, *We Are Not Afraid*, p. 2.

19. Quoted in Huie, *Three Lives for Mississippi*, p. 76.

20. Quoted in *Mississippi Black Paper*, p. 66.

21. Quoted in Huie, *Three Lives for Mississippi*, p. 90.

Chapter Two: The Search

22. Quoted in *Newsweek*, "The Invaders," p. 26.

23. Quoted in *Time*, "A Crime Called Conspiracy," December 11, 1964, p. 30.

24. Quoted in Cagin and Dray, *We Are Not Afraid*, p. 319.

25. Quoted in Winstead, *Back to Mississippi*, p. 251.

26. Quoted in Cagin and Dray, *We Are Not Afraid*, p. 327.

27. Quoted in Winstead, *Back to Mississippi*, p. 251.

28. Quoted in Hampton and Fayer, *Voices of Freedom*, p. 191.

29. Quoted in Winstead, *Back to Mississippi*, p. 251.

30. Quoted in Cagin and Dray, *We Are Not Afraid*, p. 362.

31. Quoted in Huie, *Three Lives for Mississippi*, p. 124.

32. Quoted in Erenrich, *Freedom Is a Constant Struggle*, p. 366.

Chapter Three: The Discovery

33. *Time*, "The Search," July 10, 1964, p. 27.

34. Quoted in Cagin and Dray, *We Are Not Afiaid*, p. 371.

35. Quoted in Cagin and Dray, *We Are Not Afraid*, p. 374.

36. Quoted in Huie, *Three Lives for Mississippi*, p. 136.

37. Quoted in Huie, *Three Lives for Mississippi*, p. 130.

38. Quoted in Cagin and Dray, *We Are Not Afraid*, p. 371.

39. Quoted in Huie, *Three Lives for Mississippi*, p. 133.

40. Quoted in Cagin and Dray, *We Are Not Afraid*, p. 367.

41. Quoted in Winstead, *Back to Mississippi*, p. 230.

42. Quoted in *Time*, "Grim Discovery in Mississippi," August 14, 1964, p. 17.

43. Quoted in *Time*, "Grim Discovery in Mississippi," p. 17.

Chapter Four: Confessions

44. Quoted in Winstead, *Back to Mississippi*, p. 229.

45. Maryanne Vollers, *Ghosts of Mississippi*. Boston: Little, Brown, 1995, p. 221.

46. Quoted in Cagin and Dray, *We Are Not Afraid*, p. 432.

47. Quoted in Cagin and Dray, *We Are Not Afraid*, p. 280.

48. Quoted in *Time*, "Time of Trial," October 20, 1967, p. 22.

49. Quoted in Erenrich, *Freedom Is a Constant Struggle*, p. 349.

50. Quoted in Erenrich, *Freedom Is a Constant Struggle*, p. 349.

51. Quoted in *Newsweek*, "The Philadelphia

Murders," October 23, 1967, p. 33.

52. Quoted in Erenrich, *Freedom Is a Constant Struggle*, p. 350.

53. Quoted in Erenrich, *Freedom Is a Constant Struggle*, p. 352.

54. Quoted in Chaney, "The Struggle for Justice," p. 3+.

55. Quoted in *Time*, "A Crime Called Conspiracy," p. 30.

Chapter Five: The Trial

56. Quoted in *Time*, "A Crime Called Conspiracy," p. 29.

57. Quoted in Cagin and Dray, *We Are Not Afraid*, p. 436.

58. Quoted in Winstead, *Back to Mississippi*, p. 221.

59. Quoted in *Time*, "Strategic Retreat," December 18, 1964, p. 23.

60. Quoted in *Time*, "True to Form," March 5, 1965, p. 25.

61. Quoted in Winstead, *Back to Mississippi*, p. 258.

62. Quoted in Cagin and Dray, *We Are Not Afraid*, p. 446.

63. Quoted in Huie, *Three Lives for Mississippi*, p. 153.

64. Quoted in Winstead, *Back to Mississippi*, p. 260.

65. Quoted in Cagin and Dray, *We Are Not Afraid*, pp. 446–447.

66. Quoted in Cagin and Dray, *We Are Not Afraid*, p. 449.

67. Quoted in Huie, *Three Lives for Mississippi*, p. 159.

68. Quoted in Cagin and Dray, *We Are Not Afraid*, p. 450.

Afterword: Justice Delayed

69. Quoted in James Dickerson, *Dixie's Dirty Secret*. Armonk, NY: M.E. Sharpe, 1998, p. 151.

70. Quoted in Vollers, *Ghosts of Mississippi*, p. 228.

71. Quoted in Huie, *Three Lives for Mississippi*, p. 160.

72. Quoted in Chaney, "The Struggle for Justice," p. 3+.

73. Quoted in Winstead, *Back to Mississippi*, p. 289.

74. Quoted in James Dao, "Indictment Makes Start at Lifting a 40-Year-Old Cloud Over a Mississippi County," *New York Times*, January 8, 2005.

75. Quoted in Rosalind Bentley, "Prosecution Rests in '64 Murder Case," *Atlanta Journal-Constitution*, June 19, 2005.

76. Quoted in *CBS News*, "Miss. Burning Jury Faces Impasse," www.cbsnews.com/stories/2005/06/21/national/main703292_page2.shtml.

77. Quoted in Harriet Ryan, "Jurors Announce They Are Split 6-to-6 in

Klansman's Triple-Murder Trial," *Court TV*, www.courttv.com/trials/killen/0623005-pm_ctv.html.

78. Quoted in Harriet Ryan, "Ex-Klansman Receives 60 Years for Three 1964 Kill-ings," *Court TV*, www.court tv.com/trials/killen/062305_sentence_ctv.html.

79. Quoted in Claude Lewis, "Mississippi Learning: Justice Is Slow, But Sure," *Philadelphia Inquirer*, June 29, 2005.

For Further Reading

Books

Michael Barone and Richard E. Cohen, *The Almanac of American Politics 2006*. Washington, DC: National Journal, 2005. Information about the fifty states historically, culturally, and politically. Includes demographic information on Mississippi and how it has changed since the 1960s.

Seth Cagin and Philip Dray, *We Are Not Afraid*. New York: Macmillan, 1988. A thorough, well-written account of the Freedom Summer killings through the 1967 trial. Includes valuable background information about civil rights, the Ku Klux Klan, and Neshoba County.

James Dickerson, *Dixie's Dirty Secret*. Armonk, NY: M.E. Sharpe, 1998. About the civil rights era in the South, with some attention paid to the Freedom Summer murder case.

Susie Erenrich, ed., *Freedom Is a Constant Struggle*. Montgomery, AL: Black Belt Press, 1999. An anthology of song lyrics, reminiscences, artwork, and speeches relating to the civil rights movement in Mississippi. Only a few entries in this large volume deal directly with the Freedom Summer murder case, but there is plenty of useful information here about the civil rights movement and Mississippi in general.

Henry Hampton and Steve Fayer, *Voices of Freedom*. New York: Bantam Books, 1990. A long and informative collection of first-person accounts from the civil rights movement. Several of the accounts pertain directly to the Freedom Summer movement and to the killings of Goodman, Schwerner, and Chaney.

William Bradford Huie, *Three Lives for Mississippi*, rev. ed. New York: Signet, 1968. Huie, a journalist from Alabama, was horrified—but not surprised—when he heard that Goodman, Schwerner, and Chaney had disappeared. This book, originally published in 1965, presents the basic outline of the three men's disappearance and the discovery of the bodies; the revised edition includes an afterword about the 1967 trial and the events leading up to it.

Doug McAdam, *Freedom Summer*. New York: Oxford University Press, 1988. A scholarly look at the Freedom Summer, focusing particularly on the volunteers' reasons for going to Mississippi and their experiences in the state.

Mississippi Black Paper. New York: Random House, 1965. This volume includes almost sixty first-person accounts of brutality and discrimination in Mississippi, collected from reports given by whites and blacks alike. Includes Rita Schwerner's account of the activities she and her husband undertook in Meridian and her description of the disappearance of the three men in Neshoba County.

Maryanne Vollers, *Ghosts of Mississippi*. Boston: Little, Brown, 1995. About the killing of civil rights leader Medgar Evers and the aftermath of that case; frequently discusses conditions in Mississippi during the 1960s and touches on the Freedom Summer case as well.

Mary Winstead, *Back to Mississippi*. New York: Hyperion, 2002. Winstead grew up in Minnesota, but her father was a native of Neshoba County, Mississippi; his family was related to Edgar Ray Killen. This is Winstead's memoir, a well-written, interesting book in which the Freedom Summer killings play a major role.

Periodicals

Rosalind Bentley, "Prosecution Rests in '64 Murder Case," *Atlanta Journal-Constitution*, June 19, 2005.

Ben Chaney, "The Struggle for Justice," *Human Rights*, Spring 2000.

James Dao, "Indictment Makes Start at Lifting a 40-Year-Old Cloud Over a Mississippi County," *The New York Times*, January 8, 2005.

Gerald W. Johnson, "Judgment in Mississippi," *New Republic*, December 26, 1964.

Danielle Knight, "Trying Times," *U.S. News and World Report*, June 27, 2005.

Claude Lewis, "Mississippi Learning: Justice Is Slow, But Sure," *Philadelphia Inquirer*, June 29, 2005.

Jarrett Murphy, "Still Digging," *Village Voice*, February 2–8, 2005.

Newsweek, "The Philadelphia Murders," October 23, 1967.

Time, "Cooling the Controversy," December 11, 1964.

Time, "A Crime Called Conspiracy," December 11, 1964.

Time, "Grim Discovery in Mississippi," August 14, 1964.

Time, "No Federal Case?" March 8, 1965.

Time, "Reckoning in Meridian," October 27, 1967.

Time, "The Search," July 10, 1964.

Time, "Strategic Retreat," December 18, 1964.

Time, "Time of Trial," October 20, 1967.

Time, "Toward Outlawing Murder," April 8, 1966.

Time, "True to Form," March 5, 1965.

Internet Sources

CBS News, "Miss. Burning Jury Faces Impasse," http://www.cbs news.com/stories/2005/06/21/national/main703292_page2.shtml.

Harriet Ryan, "Ex-Klansman Receives 60

Years for Three 1964 Killings," *Court TV.* www.courttv.com/trials/killen/062 305-sentence_ctv_html.

Harriet Ryan, "Jurors Announce They Are Split 6-to-6 in Klansman's Triple-Murder Trial," *Court TV.* www.courttv.com/trials/killen/ 062005_pm-ctv.html.

Web Sites

Congress on Racial Equality, "Chaney, Goodman, and Schwerner" (www.core-online.org/history/chaney.htm). This organization, one of the sponsors of the Freedom Summer project, continues to be active in working for civil rights. This page includes information about the three civil rights workers and what happened to them in 1964.

Court TV, "Civil Rights Murder Case," (www.courttv.com/trials/killen/index.html). An index page providing links to articles about the 2005 murder trial of Edgar Ray Killen, including background on the case.

Federal Bureau of Investigation, "MIBURN," (foia.fbi.gov/foiaindex/miburn.htm). Excerpts from the original files kept by the FBI in connection with the Freedom Summer murder case. Many sections of the originals are blacked out, and the pages can be difficult to manage because they are PDF files; still, a fascinating resource.

James Earl Chaney Foundation (www.jecf.org/index.html). This organization, founded by James Chaney's younger brother Ben, seeks to carry on the work of earlier civil rights activists. The site includes information about the three civil rights workers and their murders.

"The Mississippi Burning Trial" (www.law.umkc.edu/faculty/projects/ftrials/price&bowers/price&bowers.htm). This site contains newspaper articles, excerpts from the trial, and other material relating to the Freedom Summer case, including information about the three civil rights workers, Justice Department official John Doar, and the Ku Klux Klan members charged with the killings.

WhiteHouseTapes.org, "Mississippi Burning 1964" (www.whitehousetapes.org/exhibits/miss_burning/). A collection of transcripts and audio files relating to President Lyndon Johnson's phone conversations soon after the disappearance of the three civil rights workers. A fascinating look at one aspect of the Freedom Summer case.

Index

Picture Credits

About the Author

Stephen Currie is the author of more than forty books, including a number of works on history and some historical fiction. Among his books for Lucent are *Life in a Wild West Show*, *The Olympic Games*, and *Adoption*. He is also a teacher. He grew up in Illinois and now lives with his family in upstate New York.